Thoughts on Family Worship

by

James W. Alexander
Pastor of the Duane St. Presbyterian Church, New York

Edited by Rev. Don Kistler

Soli Deo Gloria Publications
. . . for instruction in righteousness . . .

Soli Deo Gloria Publications
P.O. Box 451, Morgan, PA 15064
(412) 221-1901/ FAX 221-1902

*

Thoughts on Family Worship was first published in
1847 by the Presbyterian Board of Publication.
This Soli Deo Gloria reprint, in which
grammar, spelling, and formatting
changes have been made, is
© 1998 by Don Kistler
and Soli Deo Gloria.

*

ISBN 1-57358-081-3

Contents

Preface

Although this is but a small book, there may be some by whom it will be thought too large for its subject. Such persons must differ in their estimate of domestic religion from the writer, who has been impelled to study the institution by a profound conviction of its value. In a period when the world is every day making new inroads into the church, it has especially invaded the household. Our church cannot compare with that of the seventeenth century in this regard. Along with Sabbath observance and the catechizing of children, family worship has lost ground. There are many heads of families, communicants in our churches, and, according to a scarcely credible report, some ruling elders and deacons who maintain no stated daily service of God in their dwellings. It is to awaken such to their duty that this volume has been prepared.

The richest inheritance which some of us have is the domestic rite, which has been in our houses as far back as record or tradition goes. A venerable parishioner of the author's has enjoyed family worship with no less than six generations, including a grandfather and great-grand-children. Let other heirlooms perish, but let us not deny to our offspring the worship of that God who has been our dwelling-place in all generations.

While the chapters which ensue are anything but controversial, they have not been written on any scheme of compromise. As issued by the Presbyterterian Board of Publication, they need no apology for containing Presbyterian doctrine, and a decided and affectionate allusion to the history and usages of our church.

Valuable extracts have been made from several books on the subject of prayer, and from none more largely than from a little tract entitled "The Church in the House," by Rev. James Hamilton of London.

If it should please the adorable Head of the Church to make this book instrumental in extending the domestic worship of God's people, and especially in arousing the children of the covenant to honor the God of their fathers, it will be to this writer an unspeakable satisfaction. With earnest desires and prayers for this, I submit it to the members of that venerable and beloved church in which my fathers were reared, and in which I desire my children to abide.

James W. Alexander
New York
June 15, 1847

1

The Nature, Warrant, and History of Family Worship

Family worship, as the name imports, is the joint worship rendered to God by all the members of one household.

There are some duties so plain that they are rather assumed than commanded in the Word of God; and the number of such is greater than might be supposed on a superficial examination. This is especially true of those duties which belong to the family relation, as, for example, those of the mother to her baby. They are subjected to regulation and are objects of frequent allusion, but are not incorporated into the law of commandments. We are not to wonder, therefore, if we find, even in the New Testament, no separate and explicit injunction to worship God in the family. As little do we find any command to pray when we preach the Word, or when death has visited our dwellings. These are things which it was safe to leave with the pious sentiment of Christians; and yet they are no less characteristic of good men, nor less universal in the Church.

The newborn soul must pray even as the newborn child must breathe. And wherever the grace of prayer is shed forth in the soul, it will flow out in certain acts. There is an irresistible impulse to pray for those whom we love; and not only to pray *for* them, but *with* them. There is a natural as well as a gracious prompting to pray with those who are near to us. Prayer is a social exercise. The prayer which our

Lord taught His disciples bears this stamp on every petition. It is this principle which leads to the united devotions
of church assemblies, and which immediately manifests itself in Christian families.

If there were but two human beings upon earth, they
would be drawn, if they were of sanctified hearts, to pray
with one another. Here we have the fountain of domestic
worship. Time was when there were but two human beings upon earth; and we may feel assured that they offered
adoration in common. This was the family worship of
Paradise. It is, therefore, no profane fiction, but a pious endeavor to shadow forth what undoubtedly took place when
the great poet represents Adam and Eve as addressing their
morning thoughts in concert to God:

> Soon as they forth were come to open sight
> Of dayspring and the sun, who, scarce uprisen
> With wheels yet hovering o'er the ocean brim,
> That parallel to the earth his dewy ray,
> Discovering in wide landscape all the east
> Of Paradise and Eden's happy plains,
> Lowly they bowed adoring, and began
> Their orisions, each morning duly paid
> In various style; for neither various style
> Nor holy rapture wanted they to praise
> Their Maker, in fit strains pronounced or sung
> Unmeditated, such prompt eloquence
> Flowed from their lips, in prose or numerous verse,
> More tunable than needed lute or harp
> To add more sweetness; and they thus began.
> (*Paradise Lost*, Book V:138)

That religion should especially pertain to domestic rela-
tions is not at all wonderful. The family is the oldest of
human societies; it is as old as the creation of the race. Men

were not drawn together into families by a voluntary determination or social compact according to the absurd figment of infidels; they were created in families. This has been recognized in every covenant; and the gospel, so far from destroying, has bound more closely and sanctified the family. By circumcision under the Old Testament, and by baptism under the New, God has perpetually reminded His people of the honor set on this connection.

It is not our purpose to make any ingenious efforts to force into our service the history of the Old Testament, or to search for family worship in every age of the world. That it has existed in every age I do not doubt; that the Old Testament was intended to communicate this fact is not so clear. But without any indulgence of fancy we cannot fail to discern the principle of family worship, appearing and re-appearing as a familiar thing, in the remotest periods.

While all the church of God was in the ark, the worship was plainly family worship; and after the subsiding of the waters, when "Noah builded an altar unto the Lord," it was a family sacrifice which he offered (Genesis 8:20). The patriarchs seem to have left a record of their social worship at every encampment. As soon as we find Abraham in the promised land, we find him rearing an altar in the plain of Moreh (Genesis 12:7). The same thing occurs in the vale between Hai and Bethel. Isaac not only renews the fountains which his father had opened, but keeps up his devotions, building an altar at Beersheba (Genesis 26:25). Jacob's altar at Bethel was eminently a family monument, and was signalized by his saying on the way "unto his household, and to all that were with him, 'Put away the strange gods that are among you' " (Genesis 35:1–2). The altar was named EL-BETH-EL. This descent of religious rites in the family line was in correspondence with that declaration of Jehovah respecting the family religion which would prevail in Abraham's house (Genesis 18:19). The service of Job on behalf of his children was a perpetual service; he "sent and sanctified them, and rose up early in the morning, and offered burnt-offerings according to the number of them all; thus did Job continually;" or, as it is in the Hebrew, "all the days." The book of Deuteronomy is full of family religion, as an example of which we may especially note the sixth chapter. The Passover, as we shall observe more fully in the sequel, was a family rite.

Everywhere in the Old Testament, good men take cognizance of the domestic tie in their religion. Joshua, even at the risk of being left with none but his family, will adhere to God: "As for me and my house, we will serve the Lord" (Joshua 24:15). David, after public services at the tabernacle, where, "he blessed the people in the name of the Lord," returns "to bless his household" (2 Samuel 6:18–20). He had learned to connect God's service with domestic bonds in the house of his father Jesse, where there was "a yearly sacrifice for all the family" (1 Samuel 20:6). And in the predictions of penitential humbling, which shall take place when God pours on the house of David and the inhabitants of Jerusalem, the spirit of grace and of supplications, the suitableness of such exercises to families, as such, is not overlooked. "The land shall mourn, every family apart; the family of David apart, and their wives apart; the family of Nathan apart, and their wives apart; the family of Levi apart, and their wives apart; the family of Shimei apart, and their wives apart; all the families that remain, apart, and their wives apart" (Zechariah 12:12–14).

The modern Jews in every part of the world keep up a domestic service. In their liturgy this is provided for, at least as voluminously as in any Christian ritual. As the subject is seldom treated, a few additional particulars will not be out of place; and though these relate primarily to the German and Polish Jews, they are substantially true of all others. The Hebrew liturgy fills six or seven volumes. One of these is devoted to the daily prayers. They are read in the synagogue, but are also read at home by all who are considered devout. In the morning it is the duty of every Israelite, as soon as he rises, to wash himself and repeat a blessing. He then puts on the garment with fringes and repeats another blessing. He then proceeds with a service, including prayers, psalms, and other portions of Scripture, to which large additions are made on Sabbaths and festivals. This must all take place before breakfast.

The evening daily service, though shorter, is of the same kind. During the morning prayer, except on Sabbaths and holidays, the Jews make use of the Tephilin, or phylacteries. The extent of these devotions may be understood when we add that, for the Sabbath, they occupy more than fifty octavo pages. [This statement is made on the authority of Mr. Henry Goldsmith, a learned Israelite, and professor of the Hebrew language in New York. See also the "Form of Daily Prayers, according to the custom of the German and Polish Jews, as read in their Synagogues, and used in their Families," published in London.]

In the New Testament, the traces of family religion are not less obvious. We gladly borrow the animated language of Mr. Hamilton of London, and ask: "Do you envy Cornelius, whose prayers were heard, and to whom the Lord sent a special messenger to teach him the way of salvation? He was a 'devout man, one who feared God with all his house, and prayed to God always'; and who was so anxious for the salvation of his family, that he got together his kinsmen and near friends, that they might be ready to hear the apostle when he arrived, and share with himself the benefit (Acts 10:2, 24, 31). Do you admire Aquila and Priscilla, Paul's 'helpers in Christ Jesus,' and who were so skillful in the Scriptures that they were able to teach a young minister the way of God more perfectly? You will find that one reason for their familiarity with the Scriptures was that they had a 'church in their house' " (Acts 18:26; Romans 16:5). It was doubtless recognized in regard to spiritual as well as in regard to temporal things that "if any provide not for his own, and especially for those of his own household, he hath denied the faith, and is worse than an infidel" (1 Timothy 5:8). That spirit of social prayer which led disciples to join in supplication or praise in upper chambers, in prisons, in the stocks, and on the sea beach (Acts 1:13, 16:25; Galatians 4:12; 2 Timothy 1:3) could not but have manifested itself in daily household devotion.

Our records of primitive Christianity are so much distorted and corrupted by a superstitious tradition that we need not be surprised to find a simple and spiritual service such as this thrown into the shade by sacerdotal rites. Yet we discern enough to teach us that believers of the first ages were not neglectful of family worship. Many of the authorities cited by Bishop Mant in his work on *Daily Prayer* are quite as cogent in favor of a domestic service as of a daily office in the church edifice, which some are so zealously reviving.

"In general," says Augustus Neander in a work not published among us, "they followed the Jews in observing the three seasons of day, nine, twelve, and three o'clock, as special hours of prayer; yet they did not use these in a legal manner such as militated against Christian liberty; for Tertullian says, in regard to times of prayer, 'nothing is prescribed except that we may pray at every hour and in every place.' The Christians began and closed the day with prayer. Before meals, before the bath, they prayed; for, as Tertullian says, the 'refreshment and nourishment of the soul must precede the refreshment and nourishment of the body; the heavenly before the earthly.' When a Christian from abroad, after brotherly reception and hospitality in the house of a brother Christian, took his leave, he was dismissed from the Christian family with prayer because, said they, 'in thy brother thou hast beheld thy Lord.' For every affair of ordinary life they made preparation by prayer" (*Denfwurbigfeiten*, ii:83).

To this we may add the statements of a learned man who has made Christian antiquities his peculiar study. "Instead of consuming their leisure hours in vacant idleness, or deriving their chief amusement from boisterous merriment, the recital of tales of superstition, or the chanting of the profane songs of the heathen, they passed their hours of repose in rational and enlivening pursuits; they found pleasure in enlarging their religious knowledge, and entertainment in songs that were dedicated to the praise of God. These formed their pastime in private, and their favorite recreations at their family and friendly meetings. With their minds full of the inspiring influence of these, they returned with fresh ardor to their scenes of toil; and to gratify their taste for a renewal of these, they longed for release from labor far more than to appease their appetite with the provisions of the table. Young women sitting at the distaff, and matrons going about the duties of the household, were constantly humming some spiritual airs. And Jerome relates that where he lived one could not go into the field without hearing the ploughman at his hallelujahs, the mower at his hymns, and the vinedresser singing the Psalms of David. It was not merely at noon or at mealtime that the primitive Christians read the Word of God and sang praises to His name. At an early hour in the morning, the family was assembled and a portion of Scripture was read from the Old Testament, which was followed by a hymn and a prayer in which thanks were offered up to the Almighty for preserving them during the silent watches of the night, and for His goodness in permitting them to meet in health of body and soundness of mind. At the same time His grace was implored to defend them amid the dangers and temptations of the day, to make them faithful to every duty, and to enable them in all respects to walk worthy of their Christian vocation. In the evening, before retiring to rest, the family again assembled; the same form of worship was observed as in the morning except that the service was considerably protracted beyond the period which could conveniently be allotted to it in the commencement of the day. Besides all these observances, they were in the habit of rising at midnight to engage in prayer and the singing of psalms, a practice of venerable antiquity, and which, as Dr. Cave justly supposes, took its origin from the first times of persecution when, not daring to meet together in the day, they were forced to keep their religious assemblies in the night" (*The Antiquities of the Christian Church,* by Rev. Lyman Coleman, second edition, p. 375).

When we come down to the revival of evangelical piety at the Reformation, we find ourselves in the midst of such a stream of authority and example that we must content ourselves with general statements. Whatever may be the practice of their degenerate sons, the early Reformers are universally known to have set great value on family devotion. The prayers of Luther in his house are recorded with warmth by his coevals and biographers. The churches of Germany, in a better day, were blessed with a wide prevalence of household piety. Similar facts are recorded of Switzerland, France, and Holland.

But in no country has the light of the dwelling burned more brightly than in Scotland. Family worship, in all its fullness, was coeval with the first reformation period. Probably no land, in proportion to its inhabitants, ever had so many praying families; probably none has so many now. In 1647, the General Assembly issued a *Directory for Family Worship,* in which they speak as follows:

> The ordinary duties comprehended under the exercise of piety, which should be in families when they are convened to that effect, are these: first, prayer and praises, performed with a special reference as well to the condition of the Kirk of God and this kingdom as to the present state of the family and every member thereof. Next, reading of the Scriptures, with catechizing in a plain way, that the understandings of the simpler may be the better enabled to profit under the public ordinances, and they made more capable to understand the Scriptures when they are read; together with godly conferences tending to the edification of all the members in the most holy faith; as also, admonition and rebuke, upon just reasons, from those who have authority in the family. The head of the family is to take care that none of the family withdraw himself from any part of family worship; and seeing the ordinary performance of all the parts of family worship belongeth properly to the head of the family, the minister is to stir up such as are lazy, and train up such as are weak, to a fitness for these exercises. So many as can conceive prayer ought to make use of that gift of God; albeit those who are rude and weaker may begin at a set form of

prayer; but so that they be not sluggish in stirring up in themselves (according to their daily necessities) the spirit of prayer, which is given to all the children of God in some measure; to which effect they ought to be more fervent and frequent in secret prayer to God, for enabling of their hearts to conceive and their tongues to express convenient desires to God for their family. These exercises ought to be performed in great sincerity, without delay, laying aside all exercises of worldly business or hindrances, notwithstanding the mockings of atheists and profane men; in respect of the great mercies of God to this land, and of His corrections, whereby lately He has exercised us. And to this effect, persons of eminency, and all elders of the kirk, not only ought to stir up themselves and families to diligence herein, but also to concur effectually that in all other families, where they have power and charge, the said exercises be conscionably performed.

The faithfulness of private Christians, in regard to this duty, was made a matter of inquiry by church courts. In 1596 the Act of Assembly ratified December 17–18, 1638, among other provisions for the visitation of churches, by presbyteries, the following questions were proposed to the heads of families: "Do the elders visit the families within the quarter and bounds assigned to each of them? Are they careful to have the worship of God set up in the families of their bounds?" The minister also is directed in his pastoral visits to ask, 'Whether God be worshipped in the family, by prayers, praises, and reading of the Scriptures? Concerning the behavior of servants towards God and towards man; if they attend family and public worship? If there be catechizing in the family?" (Recited in *Overtures of General Assembly, A. D. 1705, concerning the method of proceeding in*

Kirk-Sessions and Presbyteries).

When the *Confession of Faith* of the Westminster Assembly of Divines was adopted by the Church of Scotland, it contained this provision, which is still valid among ourselves: "God is to be worshipped everywhere in spirit and in truth; as in private families daily, and in secret each one by himself" (xxi:6). In conformity with these principles, the practice of family worship became universal throughout the Presbyterian body in Scotland, and among all the Dissenters in England. In Scotland especially, the humblest persons in the remotest cottages honored God by daily praise; and nothing is more characteristic of the people at this day. "I have sometimes seen family worship in great houses," says Mr. Hamilton, "but I have felt that God was quite as near when I knelt with a praying family on the earthen floor of their cottage. I have known of family worship among the reapers in a barn. It used to be common in the fishing boats upon the firths and lakes of Scotland. I have heard of its being observed in the depths of a coal pit." So marked a feature in the cottage life of Scotland could not be overlooked by Burns; and happy had it been for him if he had lived more in accordance with the practice of his praying father. It has been fitly asked, "Where in Italy or Austria shall we meet anything like the 'Cotter's Saturday Night'?"

> The cheerfu' supper done, wi' serious face,
> They round the ingle form a circle wide;
> The sire turns o'er wi' patriarchal grace
> The big ha' Bible, ance his father's pride;
> His bonnet reverently is laid aside,
> His lyart haffets wearing thin and bare:
> Those strains that once did sweet in Zion glide,

He wales a portion with judicious care;
And, Let us worship God! he says with solemn air.

They chant their artless notes in simple guise,
They tune their hearts, by far their noblest aim
Perhaps Dundee's wild warbling measures rise,
Of sainted Martyrs worthy of the name,
Or noble Elgin beats the heavenward flame,
The sweetest far of Scotia's holy lays.
Compared with these Italian trills are tame;
The tickled ears no heart-felt rapture raise,
Nae unison hae they with our Creator's praise.

The priest-like father reads the sacred page,
How Abram was the friend of God on high,
Or Moses bade eternal warfare wage
With Amalek's ungracious progeny;
Or how the royal bard did groaning lie
Beneath the stroke of Heaven's avenging ire;
Or Job's pathetic plaint and wailing cry;
Or rapt Isaiah's wild seraphic fire;
Or other holy seers that tune the sacred lyre.

Perhaps the Christian volume is the theme:
How guiltless blood for guilty man was shed,
How He who bore in heaven the second name,
Had not on earth whereon to lay His head;
How His first followers and servants sped;
The precept sage they wrote to many a land:
How he who lone in Patmos banished
Saw in the sun a mighty angel stand;
And heard great Babylon's doom pronounced by heaven's
    command.

Then kneeling down to heaven's eternal King,
The saint, the father, and the husband prays,
Hope springs exulting on triumphant wing,
That thus they all shall meet in future days:
There ever bask in uncreated rays,

No more to sigh or shed the bitter tear,
Together hymning their Creator's praise,
In such society, yet still more dear;
While circling time moves round in an eternal sphere.

Compared with this, how poor religion's pride,
In all the pomp of method and of art,
When men display to congregations wide,
Devotion's every grace except the heart;
The Power incensed the pageant will desert,
The pompous strain, the sacerdotal stole;
But haply in some cottage far apart,
May hear well-pleased the language of the soul,
And in His book of life the inmates poor enroll.

The excellency of this picture is that it contains not a stroke of fiction. Such scenes are presented week after week among the Scottish peasantry. They are such as the Presbyterians of America have known from the days of childhood. Nor were they alone in this unspeakable privilege. The fathers of New England, having drunk into the same spirit, left the same legacy to their sons.

It is highly honorable to family worship, as a spiritual service, that it languishes and goes into decay in times when error and worldliness make inroads upon the church. This has remarkably been the case among some of the Protestant communities of the continent of Europe. As a general statement, it must be said that family worship is not so extensively practiced there, and of course it cannot be so highly prized as in the churches of Great Britain and America. This is true even when the comparison is made between those in the respective countries whose attachment to the gospel appears to be the same. There are many, especially in France and Switzerland, who as highly value, and as regularly maintain, the daily worship of God as any of their brethren in England or the United States; but they constitute exceptions to the above statement rather than any refutation of it. Christian travelers observe, however, that better views on this subject, as on the observance of the Sabbath, are decidedly on the increase in France and Switzerland, and probably, to a certain extent, in Germany and other countries on the Continent. This is to be attributed to the translation of many excellent works from the English into French, and their circulation in those countries within the last few years. (For valuable testimony on this point, I am indebted to my friend, the Rev. Robert Baird, D. D., than whom no man can be a more competent witness.)

From what has been said, it is manifest that the universal voice of the Church in its best periods has been in favor of family worship. The reason for this has also become apparent. It is a service due to God, in regard to His bountiful and gracious relation to families as such, rendered necessary by the wants, temptations, dangers, and sins of the family state; it in the highest degree fit and right from the facilities afforded for maintaining it by the very condition of every household. Of its benefits, it is our purpose to speak in the ensuing chapters.

For the sake of method, we shall consider the influence of this institution on individual piety, on parents, children, and domestics; in regard to intellectual improvement, internal harmony, and the sanctified use of chastisements, and on visitors and neighbors. We shall examine its influence on the preservation of sound doctrine, on the church, the commonwealth, and posterity; and, after some practical suggestions towards the due performance of the duty, we shall urge our readers, in the fear of God, to undertake it without delay.

2

The Influence of Family Worship on Individual Piety

From the moment when we first repeat the Lord's Prayer, saying "Our Father," we are taught that our religion is social. It not only influences others, but is exercised and enjoyed in common with others. What a monstrous thing it would be for a man to spend a lifetime in the midst of fellow beings without ever feeling or acting towards them in a religious capacity! We can scarcely conceive of true light as being so hidden under a bushel. Solitary experience like this would be worse then monkery, for that is social; worse than the seclusion of the anchoret, for that is removed from witnesses. Where the Spirit of God really operates on a soul, He brings it into fellowship with other renewed souls and renders it a center of radiance to all around.

If this is true of the great body of men, it is more eminently true of the family group. In religion, "it is not good for man to be alone." The experience of the heart is the grand thing, and this is best promoted in the secrecy of the closet; yet it must not, and cannot, abide in the closet or the heart, but will be like "the ointment of the right hand, which bewrayeth itself," like the alabaster box of fragrance that fills all the house. Love, which is the great manifestation of grace, is too communicative in its nature to be always pent up. The electric current will pervade all whose

hands are joined in the domestic circle. They will feel together, read God's Word together, sing together, and pray
together; and it is indispensable that there should be some
established mode of cherishing and evincing this fellowship
of experience.

While we should all beware of that species of religion
which has no privacy, and which lives only on the excitements and sympathies of social ordinances, we should not,
therefore, overlook the legitimate influence of united prayer
and praise. Single coals die out; when drawn together, they
break into a flame. If closet worship is more solemn and
lowly, family worship may be more elevated and affectionate. Especially where the head of the family is one who
grows in grace and Christian knowledge, he will, by his
very presence, lift up the hearts of his household. The
child, the servant, and the guest will be carried up to higher
advances of devout feeling by one who has so far out-
stripped them in the flight.

Summon a family to the worship of God at stated
hours and you summon each one to a seriousness of reflection of which he might have been wholly robbed by the
hurry of the day's business. He who perhaps neglects all
private perusal of the Scriptures is constrained to hear a
portion read by one whom he reveres. He who prays but
formally, or prays not at all, in his chamber finds himself in
this sacred hour kneeling among a reverent company, and
is prompted by the ardent words of supplication to lift up
his heart unto the Lord.

There is no member of a household whose individual
piety is of such importance to all the rest as the father or
head; and there is no one whose soul is so directly influenced by the exercise of domestic worship. Where the head
of a family is lukewarm or worldly, he will send the chill

through the whole house; and if any happy exception occurs, and one or another surpasses him in faithfulness, it will be in spite of his evil example. He who ought, by his instructions and life, to afford a perpetual incitement to his inferiors and his juniors, is made to feel, in case of such delinquency, that they must look elsewhere for guidance, even if they do not weep in secret places over his neglects. Where the head of the family is a man of faith, affection, and zeal, consecrating all his works and life to Christ, it is very rare to find all his household otherwise-minded. Now one of the chief means of promoting such individual graces in the head is this his daily exercise of devotion with the members. It is more to him than to others. It is he who presides and directs in it, who selects and delivers the precious Word, and who leads the common supplication, confession, and praise. To him it is equal to an additional act of personal devotion in the day; but it is more: it is an act of devotion in which his affection and duty to his house are particularly brought before his mind; and in which he stands in the place and pleads the cause of all that he holds dearest upon earth. No one need wonder, then, that we place family prayer among the most important means of reviving and maintaining the piety of him who conducts it. I shall look at this topic in its more special reference to the parent and the master.

Observation shows that families which have no household worship are at a low ebb in spiritual things; that families where it is performed in a cold, sluggish, negligent, or hurried way are little affected by it, and little affected by any means of grace. But families where God is worshipped, every morning and evening, by all the inmates of the house in a solemn and affectionate service, are blessed with increase of piety and happiness. Every individual is blessed.

Each one receives a portion of the heavenly food.

Half the defects and transgressions of our days arise from want of consideration. Hence the unspeakable value of an exercise which twice every day calls each member of the household at least to think of God. Even the most careless or impious son or servant must now and then be forced to talk a little with conscience, and meditate a little on judgment, when the gray-haired father, bowed before God with trembling voice, pours out strong supplication and prayer. How much more mighty must be the influence on that larger number who in ten thousand Christian families in the land are more or less impressed with the importance of divine things! And how peculiar and tender and forming must the same influence be on those of the domestic group who worship God in the spirit, and who often wipe the gushing tear as they rise from their knees and look around on husband, father, mother, brother, sister, or child—all remembered in the same devotion, all clouded with the same incense of intercession!

Perhaps among our readers more than one can say: "Times without number have I felt the influence of domestic worship on my own soul. When yet a child, no one means of grace, public or private, so awakened my attention as when the children were prayed for day by day. In wayward youth, I was never so stung by conviction of my sin as when my honored father earnestly sought God for our salvation. When at length in infinite mercy I first began to open the ear to instruction, no prayer so reached my heart or so expressed my deep affections as those which were uttered by my honored father."

The gospel has this great precedence of all other systems, that it is preached to the poor. If mankind in general finds good in religion, the poor and wretched find in it peculiar good. This is true of all means and ordinances; and it is eminently true of family worship. We have often had occasion to observe this in the case of those who earn their bread by labor. The working man often has little disposal of his own time, and little privacy for religious acts. He rises, it may be, long before day, and in a wintry morning hastily prepares himself to join others in labor. He is therefore under a very strong inducement to abridge—if not omit—the Scriptures and prayer. It is of immense value for one in such circumstances to be bound by the sweet-yet-constraining tie of a family-covenant, to redeem time and call his household together for God's praise. Such acts of domestic worship are among the sweetest enjoyments of the poor man's life. He thus has ensured to him a stock of truth for the reflections of the whole day. The son and daughter who go forth to shop or factory labor carry with them some remembrance of God. And when, after a day of honorable toil, they re-assemble in the evening with the expectation of a similar service, it is to enjoy a means of grace which furnishes each individual with a new impulse towards the goal.

Those who unite every day in solemn acts of worship are thus brought to a comparison of themselves with a certain standard. They are made to recognize themselves, and to recognize one another as servants of God. It is not unnatural, therefore, that each one should sometimes be led at such a moment to say to himself, "What is this? In what character am I appearing? I am professing to honor God; but how does this comport with what I have been doing, saying, thinking, or omitting this day?" Such an aid to self-culture is not to be despised. True, the same holds good in regard to public worship and ordinances; but this is a daily ordinance, an oft-repeated influence; and it is by the manna which falls every day at the door of the tent that our souls are kept alive.

We all know that there is such a thing as sacramental, sabbath, or periodic religion, a habit of mind to be put on and off like the habit of the body. Family worship has a direct and manifest tendency to make religion a matter of every-day interest. He who appears before God twice a day, with his nearest friends and familiars, cannot easily fail to acknowledge his need of "a real business-change in the heart, and in the principle of acting" (Thomas Chalmers). Suppose him, during the day, to have slidden into the ways of a most slippery world, to have spoken unadvisedly with his lips, to have broken into wrath, or to have strained a point of integrity in buying or selling; when he comes home to his evening devotions, he must be a seared worldling or a double-masked hypocrite if he does not admit some compunction, and resolve on some amendment.

Family worship furnishes a means of making increased graces in the head of the household available to the benefit of the members. It is not every sincere servant of Christ who has the gift of free and acceptable and impressive discourse on divine subjects; though the attainment should be sought by all. The hindrances are various: lack of education, consciousness of small attainment, slowness of speech, natural diffidence, inexcusable pride or false shame, and a sense of inconsistency in the life. These causes may operate to keep the father of a family in a state of inactive insulation. Nothing tends so directly to break a channel for right influences, in this respect, as the regular and faithful observance of domestic worship. A word fitly spoken at such a time is an apple of gold. A psalm, rightly chosen and sung with the spirit and understanding, may bear up all hearts to

God. A prayer "in the Holy Ghost," though issuing from one who has not the lips of the eloquent, may go more deeply into the soul of the prodigal son or the careless neighbor than all the sermons of the year. These are influences which are undervalued because they are not singly powerful, yet when constant they are mighty; they drop as the rain and distill as the dew, "as the small rain upon the tender herb, and as the showers upon the grass." In the day of judgment and revelation, it will perhaps appear, in the case of many, that they have owed more in regard of individual piety to the operation of family religion than to any single class of causes.

In reckoning the influence of domestic worship, we must reflect that, aside from anything peculiar, it is just so much added to all the other institutions of religion. It comes day after day, and for a lifetime. I have before my mind's eye "an old disciple," the son of an old disciple. This ancient servant of God, now eighty-four years of age, has enjoyed this means of instruction and elevation since he was competent to receive any impression, more than fifty thousand times. Let no one smile at the arithmetic of the statement; it will come home to all the children of the church in the day when "after a long time, the lord of those servants cometh and reckoneth with them" (Matthew 25:19).

But we have conceded too much. Family worship has striking peculiarities of influence. Its lessons and devotions begin at the earliest period, when the infant soul is yielding as wax. Here the father or the grandfather, or perhaps the Eunice and the Lois (2 Timothy 1:5) reach forth with the molding influence which is to last for life. These means are used in circumstances peculiarly tender, when the heart is, above all, susceptible; at the home and fireside; among objects of reverence; in the circle of love. Here, if anywhere, the individual soul will feel the Word to be "profitable for doctrine, for reproof, for correction, for instruction in righteousness" (2 Timothy 3:16). Here, if anywhere, the heart will respond to the call of devotion, and be prompted to burst forth in prayer. Here the fainting experience will plume its wings for the attempts of a higher flight; and the joys of a hidden devotion will mingle with the flames of a common altar. Can our Christian life readily sacrifice or forego the aids and comforts of such an institution? Or can he, who has received so great a blessing from the home of his boyhood, willingly deny it to his own offspring?

The truth must not be concealed, so that in order to realize these advantages from the worship of God in the household we must see to it that it is conducted in a due manner. It must not be a stated formality, however punctual or decorous. It must not be the empty expression of a life which does not exist. It must be approached as if we were going to the very feet of Christ. Those who have it in charge, whether fathers, mothers, the elder son, or the Levite under the roof must be in a state of preparation, and must eye the true import and design of the ordinance. Where these cautions are observed, it will never fail to be a powerful instrument in awakening, edifying, and comforting the individual soul.

3

The Influence of Family Worship on Parents

In order to educate the children of a land, we must first educate the parents; and if an institution was demanded for this special purpose it would be impossible to find one comparable to family worship. Some things which were hinted at in the foregoing chapter may here be laid open more explicitly.

The maintenance of domestic religion in every house is primarily entrusted to the head of the family, whoever this may be. If he is totally unfit for the charge by an unbelieving mind or an ungodly life, the consideration is one which should startle and appall him; and it is affectionately submitted to any reader whose conscience may plead guilty to such an imputation. There are instances where divine grace has so endowed someone in the household, even though not the parent or the senior, as plainly to devolve on him the performance of this duty. The widowed mother, the elder sister, or the actual guardian may stand in the parent's place. But inasmuch as in a majority of cases the service, if rendered at all, must be rendered by the father, we shall treat the subject under this supposition, premising that principles laid down apply in most of their extent to all the other influences.

No man can approach the duty of leading his household in an act of devotion without solemn reflection on the place which he occupies in regard to them. He is their head. He is such by a divine and unalterable constitution.

These are duties and prerogatives which he cannot alienate.
There is something more than mere precedence in age,
knowledge, or substance. He is the father and the master.
No act of his, and nothing in his character, can fail to leave
a mark on those around him. This he will be apt to feel
when he calls them about him to pray to God; and the
more devoutly he addresses himself to the work, the more
will he feel it. Though all priesthood, in the proper sense, is
now done away on earth and absorbed in the functions of
the great High Priest, there is still something like a priestly
intervention in the service of the Christian patriarch. He is
now about to go before the little flock in the oblation of a
spiritual sacrifice of prayer and adoration. Thus it is said,
respecting Christ: "By Him, therefore, let us offer the sacrifice of praise to God continually; that is, the fruit of our
lips, giving thanks to His name" (Hebrews 13:15). This
perpetual offering the head of the family is about to make.
Until long perseverance in a deadening formality of routine
shall have blunted all sensibility, he must yield to the
solemn impression. It will sometimes lie like a burden at his
heart; it will sometimes swell within his affections, like
"wine which hath no vent" (Job 32:19).

These are salutary and elevating emotions, which go to
form the grave and lofty character which may be observed
in the old peasantry of Scotland. Though he is but a poor
and unlettered man who bows his hoary head amidst a
band of sons and daughters, yet he is more sublimely honored than prayerless kings. His head is encircled with that
"crown of glory" which is found "in the way of righteousness" (Proverbs 16:31). The father who, year after year,
presides in the sacred domestic assembly submits himself to
an influence which is incalculably strong on his own
parental character.

Where is a parent so likely to admit the impression of his responsibility as where he gathers his household for worship? It is true at all times that he is bound to watch for their souls; but now he is placed where he must feel it to be true. His family is met in a religious capacity, and is looking up to him for guidance. His eye cannot light on a single member of the group who is not committed to his especial charge. Among all these there is not one for whom he shall not give account at the judgment seat of Christ. The wife of his youth—to whom shall she look for spiritual watch if not from him? And how unnatural is the family relation when this guardianship is repudiated and this relation reversed! If the children are ever saved, it will probably be, in some degree, consequent on his exertions. Domestics, apprentices, and sojourners are all committed for a term longer or shorter to his care. The domestic minister will surely cry, "Who is sufficient for these things?" And this, most of all, when he is in the very performance of these duties. If his conscience is kept awake by personal acquaintance with God, he will never enter upon family worship without sentiments which involve this very accountability; and such sentiments cannot but have their impression on the parental character.

Unspeakable good would ensue if every father could feel himself to be the earthly-but-divinely-appointed headspring of religious influence to his household. Is it not true? And is there any means of making him feel it to be true which can be compared to the institution of family worship? Now he has assumed his rightful place as an instructor, a guide, and an exemplar in devotion. Now his mouth, even though he is a silent or a bashful man, is opened. Now he can at least rehearse the "words which the Holy Ghost speaketh," and give outlet to the gush of pent-up emotions. Perhaps some word may reach the son or the servant who has been long estranged. Perhaps some prayer, more ardent, more believing than usual, may find audience for these beloved, immortal souls. He is in the posture for seeing and for feeling these things; and that is no despicable instrument in the education of the parent, which puts him into this posture.

The hour of domestic prayer and praise is also the hour of scriptural instruction. The father has opened God's Word in the presence of his little flock. He thus admits himself to be its teacher and under-shepherd. Perhaps he is but a plain man, living by his labor, unused to schools or libraries, and, like Moses, "slow of speech and of a slow tongue." Nevertheless, he stands by the open well of wisdom and, like the same Moses, may draw water enough and water the flock (Exodus 2:19). For the time he sits "in Moses' seat," and no longer "occupieth the room of the unlearned." This is encouraging and ennobling. As the loving mother rejoices to be the fountain of nourishment to the babe which clings to her warm bosom, so the Christian father delights to convey, even by reverent reading, "the pure milk of the Word." He has found it good to his own soul, and he rejoices in an appointed means of conveying it to his offspring. Jonathan said, "See, I pray you, how mine eyes have been enlightened, because I tasted a little of this honey" (1 Samuel 14:29); and so the Christian father desires to dispense to his household that Word of the Lord which is "sweeter than honey and the honeycomb" (Psalm 19:10). The humblest master of a house may well feel himself exalted by recognizing such a relation to those who are under his care.

The example of a father is acknowledged to be all-important. The stream must not be expected to rise higher than the fountain. The Christian householder will feel himself constrained to say, "I am leading my family in solemn addresses to God; what matter of man should I be! How wise, holy, and exemplary!" This undoubtedly has been in innumerable cases the direct operation of family worship on the father. As we know that worldly men and inconsistent professors are deterred from performing this duty by the consciousness of a discrepancy between their life and any acts of devotion, so humble Christians are led by the same comparison to be more circumspect, and to order their ways in such a manner as may edify their dependents. There cannot be too many motives to a holy life, nor too many safeguards to parental example. Establish the worship of God in any house, and you erect around it a new barrier against the corruption of the world, the flesh, and the devil.

The master of the house, in family worship, appears as the intercessor for his household. The great Intercessor is indeed above, but "supplications, prayers, intercessions, and giving of thanks" (1 Timothy 2:1) are to be made below; and by whom, if not by the father for his family? The thought of this must bring solemn reflections. The parent who, with any sincerity, comes daily to implore blessings on his wife, children, and domestics will think to himself as to what they need. Here will be an urgent motive to inquire into their wants, temptations, weaknesses, errors and transgressions. The eye of a genuine father will be quick; his heart will be sensitive on these points; and the hour of devotion will gather these solicitudes together.

From such a motive, as we have already seen, holy Job, after the festivities of his children, "sent and sanctified them, and rose up early in the morning, and offered burnt-offerings, according to the number of them all; for Job said,

'It may be that my sons have sinned, and cursed God in their hearts.' Thus did Job continually" (Job 1:5). Whatever may have been the effect on the sons, the effect on Job himself was, no doubt, an awakening of mind as to his parental responsibility; and such is the effect of family worship on the head of a household.

The father of a family is under a wholesome influence when he is brought everyday to take a post of observation, and says to his own heart, "By this single means, in addition to all others, I am exerting some definite influence, good or bad, upon all who surround me. I cannot omit this service needlessly; perhaps I cannot omit it at all without detriment to my house. I cannot read the Word, I cannot sing, I cannot pray, without leaving some trace on the tender mind. How solemnly, how affectionately how believingly, should I then approach this ordinance! With how much godly fear and preparation! My conduct in this worship may save or may kill. Here is my great channel for reaching the case of those who are submitted to my charge." These are wholesome thoughts, naturally engendered by a daily ordinance which too many regard as little better than a form.

The Christian husband needs to be reminded of his obligations; he cannot be reminded of them too often. The respect, the forbearance, the love which the Scrip-tures enjoin towards the more feeble and more dependent party in the conjugal alliance, and which are the crown and glory of Christian wedlock are never more brought into action than when they who have plighted their faith to one another years ago are brought day by day to the place of prayer, and lift up a united heart at the feet of infinite mercy. As the head of every man is Christ, so the head of the woman is the man (1 Corinthians 11:3). His post is responsible in spiritual matters. He can seldom feel it more sensibly than when he falls down with the partner of his burdens at the throne of grace.

The father sees his children before him. The Word which he reads to them contains his duties to them. Whatsoever there may be of paternal affection within him must break forth at such a moment; and the frequent repetition of such sentiments must educate the heart.

The master—if I may employ a term which is in a fair way to be obsolete in our day of license and leveling—calls together his servants, and all under his control, for the worship of God. If forgetful of it at other times, he must now acknowledge and feel, at least on some occasions, that the salvation of his dependents is, to a certain extent, consigned to his care. If he can do no more, he can read God's Word to them; he can pray for them. It is not, however, the effect on the servant or child, but the effect on the master and father that we are now considering. Let any reflective mind contemplate the subject, and he will be persuaded that there must be a marked and increasing difference between the parental feelings and principles of one who habitually worships God in his family and one who worships him not. It is no trifle to have religion perpetually brought to bear upon the parental relation. In the shop, the market, the field, the highway, the office, the exchange, and even in the pulpit, the father may forget that he is a father; he cannot forget it when the curtain has dropped, when the circle draws more closely around the hearth, when the wife of his youth welcomes him to prayer, and when the eyes of his little ones are fixed on him as the minister of God to their souls. I no longer marvel that Christianity becomes a dying, empty thing in the houses of those professors (alas, that there should be such!)

where there is no joint worship of God.

In the rage for amassing wealth, which threatens the church among us, and especially in our great commercial cities, there is an estranging process going on which I fear is too little observed. Such is the insane precipitation with which the man of business rushes to his morning's task, and such the length of his absence from home, often extending till the hours of darkness, so that he gradually loses some of that parental tenderness which Providence keeps alive by the presence of those whom we love. The long continuance of such habits cannot fail to affect the character. Of all persons in the world, he should be most willing to take time for family devotions who is, by his very employment, shut out from his home most of every day. The paternal heart demands this hour of culture. A deliberate service in which the voices of infancy and age unite in praising God, amidst the flow of mutual affection, is a blessed means of countervailing the hard and selfish world which surrounds him. But above all the Christian parent needs something to keep him constantly in remembrance that his children have souls, that they look to him for more than their earthly support, and that there are means whereby, under God, he may be the instrument of their salvation. If, amidst the avocations of this life, he seldom finds time to deal faithfully with their souls; if he rarely conveys to them any sign of fear for their safety; if he is dumb in respect to Christ and eternity; here is a daily service of which the direct tendency will be to arouse him to these duties. Can it be possible for a man to pray earnestly for the salvation of his children in their hearing, representing them to God in earnest supplication as dead in trespasses and sins, while at the same time he leaves them to wonder why no syllable ever falls from his lips on those momentous subjects? The praying parent has a daily remembrancer of these and the like obligations; and while he asks heavenly good for his household, he will sometimes cry to God for grace to fulfill them. The answer of such prayers will not be withheld. The prayer-hearing God will render him a better parent, will endow him with those peculiar gifts for which, alas, professing parents are so slow to seek, and will cause him to discharge the obligations of this fearful station in a better manner, to say the least, than those who hasten through life without any token of family religion.

Prayerless parents have cause to tremble. God's anger may light upon them in their parental relation, as Eli's neglect was visited (1 Samuel 3:13). They have no right to expect parental happiness. They place themselves and their household in the defenseless condition of the heathen. "Pour out thy fury upon the heathen that know Thee not, and upon the families that call not on Thy name" (Jeremiah 10:25). Family prayer invites and bespeaks the blessing of God on all concerned, but chiefly on him who leads in it. Better a roofless house than a prayerless one; better beg one's bread with prayer than deny God by a neglect of this chief means of domestic prosperity. One who has any genuine religious faith, and any trust in God's promises, must be assured that in the rearing of his household, in providing for their support and education, in governing and restraining them, and in laboring for their souls, no good can ensue but by the blessing of God. And for this blessing, in the way of direction and grace, the Christian parent should join with his family in asking everyday. In so doing he will be not only a better man, but a better father. He will love his children more, and more wisely. He will be doubly a parent to them by the power and affection of a holy example. He will be better able to bear those reverses and bereavements which may befall him. "But how shocking is the prospect if you are determined to resist conviction and live in the willful neglect of this duty! Your families are likely to be nurseries for hell; or, if there should be an Abijah in them, 'one in whom some good thing is found toward the Lord God of Israel' (1 Kings 14:13), no thanks to you for it; you must be punished for your neglect of Him as though He had perished by your iniquity" (Samuel Davies).

4

The Influence of Family Worship on Children

There are many readers of these pages who, like the author, can go back to no period of recollection in which the worship of God was not duly observed under the parental roof; and they will agree in testifying that this is among the chief blessings for which they have to thank an ever-gracious Providence. If called upon to name the principle benefit of the institution, we should indicate its benign operation on the children of the house.

The simple fact that parents and offspring meet together every morning and evening for the Word of God and prayer is a great fact in household annals. It is the inscribing of God's name over the lintel of the door. It is the setting up of God's altar. The dwelling is marked as a house of prayer. Religion is thus made a substantive and prominent part of the domestic plan. The day is opened and closed in the name of the Lord. From the very dawn of reason, each little one grows up with a feeling that God must be honored in everything, that no business of life can proceed without Him, and that the day's work or study would be unsheltered, disorderly, and in a manner profane but for this consecration. When such a child comes in later years to mingle with families where there is no worship there is an unavoidable shudder, as if among heathen or infidel companions. In Greenland, when a stranger knocks at the door, he asks, "Is God in this house?" and if they answer, "Yes," he enters.

As prayer is the main part of all family worship, so the chief benefit to children is that they are the subjects of such prayer. As the great topic of the parent's heart is his off-spring, so they will be his great burden at the throne of grace. And what is there which the father and mother can ever do for their beloved ones that may be compared with their bearing them to God in daily supplication? And when are they so likely to do this with melting affection as when kneeling amidst the group of sons and daughters? And what prayers are more likely to be answered than those which are offered thus? The direct influence of family prayer is then to bring down the benediction of Almighty God upon the children of the house. In saying this, though we should not add another word, we adduce a sufficient and triumphant reason for the custom of our fathers. But there are incidental and collateral advantages which must not be overlooked.

Daily worship, in common, encourages children to acts of devotion. It reminds them, however giddy or care-less they may be, that God is to be adored. In many ways it suggests to them the duty and blessedness of praying for themselves. They are here familiarized with what may be called "the method of prayer," and have manifold petitions brought before their minds which may after-wards be made their own. While the favored circle is bowed before God, there is scarcely a son or daughter who will not sometimes be arrested by the voice of the father in supplication, and prompted to appropriate the petition. In many instances, we may suppose, the first believing prayers of the Christian youth ascend from the fireside. Slight impressions, otherwise transient, are thus fixed, and infant aspirations are carried up with the volume of domestic incense. Is it too much to say that, in this way, family worship becomes the means of everlasting salvation to multitudes?

The confessions, thanksgivings, and petitions of a wise householder will take their form and color from the circumstances of his house. Unless enslaved to a rigid form, he cannot but vary his requests with the changing condition of his family; and therefore he will naturally suit his words of devotion to the state of his children. It must be obvious that in this way, even when prayer is most singly directed to its proper end, a number of incidental suggestions must occur which will carry all the solemnity and pungency of exhortation, caution, and consolation. He who is prayed for will know and feel that he is prayed for. Paths of duty will be indicated; dangers will be marked; sins will be arrayed before conscience; divine blessings will be set forth as infinitely desirable. By the same means, through God's blessing, incentives to piety will be reiterated, convictions deepened, and the object of faith placed in open light. Where all this is done day by day, the heart of the child must experience some affection until it is steeled by habitual resistance.

The daily regular and solemn reading of God's holy Word by a parent before his children is one of the most powerful agencies of a Christian life. We are prone to undervalue this cause. It is a constant dropping, but it wears its mark into the rock. A family thus trained cannot be ignorant of the Word. The whole Scriptures come repeatedly before the mind. The most heedless child must observe and retain some portion of the sacred oracles; the most forgetful must treasure up some passages for life. No one part of juvenile education is more important. Between families thus instructed and those where the Bible is not read the contrast is striking. To deny such a source of influence to the youthful mind is an injustice, at the thought of which a

professor of Christianity may well tremble. The filial affections are molded by family worship. The child beholds the
parent in a peculiar relation. Nowhere is the Christian father so venerable as where he leads his house in prayer. The
tenderness of love is hallowed by the sanctity of reverence.
A chastened awe is thrown about the familiar form, and
parental dignity assumes a new and sacred aspect. There is
surely nothing unnatural in the supposition that a forward
child shall find it less easy to rebel against the rule of one
whom he daily contemplates in an act of devotion. The
children look more deeply into the parents' heart by the
medium of family prayer. A single burst of genuine fatherly
anxiety in the midst of ardent intercession may speak to the
child a volume of long-hidden and travailing grief and love.
Such words uttered on the knees, though from a plain,
untutored man, are sometimes as arrows in the heart of unconverted youth. The child is forced to say to himself,
"How can I offend against the father who daily wrestles
with God on my behalf? How can I be careless about the
soul for which he is thus concerned?" And often, when
separated from the domestic circle, has the wanderer
thought to himself, "My father and mother are now praying to God for their boy!" He is little read in the human
heart who fails to recognize here a great element of filial
piety, or who refuses to believe that the tenderness of a
child's attachment is increased by the stated worship of the
household.

There is a kindred influence upon fraternal affections.
Praying together is a certain means of attachment; those
who pray for one another cannot but love. Think of it, and
confess how impossible it is for sons and daughters everyday, during all the sunny years of youth, to bow down side
by side in common devotions and mutual intercessions

without feeling that their affection is rendered closer and holier by the very act. Brothers and sisters who have thus been led together to the throne of grace from infancy are linked by ties unknown to the rest of the world. But the topic merits a separate discussion.

Delightful as is the syllable "home," it is made tenfold more so by prayer. The ancient lares, or gods of the house, were cherished; and their altar was the domestic hearth. They were vanity and a lie: "but our God is in the heavens" (Psalm 115:3). The house of our childhood is always lovely, but the presence of the Almighty Protector makes it a sanctuary; and His altar causes home to be doubly home. However long we live, or however far we wander, it will ever abide in memory as the place of prayer, the cradle of our childlike devotions, the circle which enclosed father, mother, sister, and brother in its sacred limit. Now that which adds to the charm and the influence of home affords a mighty incentive to good and a mighty check to evil. To make a child love his home is to secure him against a thousand temptations. Families who live without God forego all such advantages and recollections. The domestic fireside no doubt has its charms, but it is shorn of its religious associations; it is less revered; and I believe it is less loved.

In families where there is daily praise of God in psalms and hymns and spiritual songs, there is an additional influence on the young. At no age are we more impressed by music, and no music is so impressive as that which is the vehicle of devotion. The little imitative creatures begin to catch the melodies long before they can understand the words. Without any exception they are delighted with this part of the service, and their proficiency is easy in proportion. No choir can be compared with that of a goodly

household, where old and young, day after day and year after year, lift up the voice in harmony. Such strains give a jo-
cund opening to the day, and cheer the harassed mind after
labor is done. Sacred song tranquilizes and softens the
mind, makes an opening for higher influences, and prepares voice and heart for the public praise of God. The
practice is the more important, as it is well known that in
order to attain its perfection the voice should be cultivated
from an early age. Nor should we omit to mention the
store of psalms and hymns which are thus treasured in the
memory. By this it is (even more than by public worship)
that the Scottish peasantry to so great an extent have the
old version of the Psalms by rote, in great part or in whole.
But this is a topic which I reserve for another place.

In the rearing of youth, nothing can be thought in-
significant which goes to train the thoughts, or gives
strength and direction to the habits. It is by a repetition of
perpetual, patient touches, small in themselves, that the
straggling branches of the vine are led by the gardener to
grow and spread aright. It is by ten thousand inappreciable
dots and scratches that the plate of the engraver is made to
represent the portrait or the landscape. So it is by an ever-
renewed application of right principles that parental care,
in the hand of sovereign grace, gives Christian habit to the
infant mind. In so precious a work nothing is unimportant; we must give heed to the minutest influences, as we
save the filings of gold and the dust of diamonds. For this
reason we ascribe to domestic worship a large share in
creating useful habits in the young. We scruple not to say
that a child receives advantage by being led to do anything,
provided it is innocent, at stated times, with frequent
repetition, and with proper care. The daily assembling of a
household, at regular periods, for a religious purpose, di-

rectly tends to promote good habits. It is a useful lesson for the speechless babe to acquire the patient stillness of the hour of prayer. It is good for a family to have a religious motive to early rising, and timely attention to personal neatness. It is something to have punctuality in the observance of two hours each day, enforced from the very dawn of life. Those who may be tempted to put this aside with a smile should first institute a comparison in regard to these particulars, between any two families of which one worships and the other does not. We are willing to abide by the results of the examination, for we are sure that in the latter will be found a great looseness of domestic arrangement, tardy rising, a slovenly toilet, a long, irregular time wasting breakfast, more conformable to the modern fashion than to Christian usage; evenings without an affectionate rally of the house; and late hours of retiring, or no fixed hours at all.

Parents who may read this book are respectfully invited to consider whether they do not owe it to their children to give them the daily worship of God. Especially are the sons and daughters of the church, whose own youth was hallowed by this constant observance, charged to recall their impressions of the past, and to reckon up the advantages which they are denying to their offspring.

Christian children must give account at the last day for the privilege of family prayer. It becomes them to be asking whether they are making use of this instrumentality. Customary means of this kind, we know, are apt to become formalities. When the family is gathered, the careless or drowsy child may hear as though he heard not, and kneel as though he knelt not; he may attend to no syllable of God's Word and join in no single petition. But let him remember that every instance of family worship affords a means of direct approach to the Most High, and thus a means of saving his soul. Blessed are those children who, early in their youthful days, remember the God of their fathers, and begin life by choosing Him as the Guide of their youth! To such, every act of worship is a solemnity and a delight, gradually ripening the soul for faithful service on earth, and for the praises of heaven. Most earnestly is it to be desired that those who have been baptized, who have been catechized, who have been, during all their youth, embraced in the circle of domestic prayer, should now, when themselves placed at the head of families, carry forward the blessed institutions in which they have been reared, and convey the words of life to coming generations. "We will not hide them from their children, showing to the generation to come the praises of the Lord, and His strength, and His wonderful works that He hath done" (Psalm 78:4).

5

Family Worship As a Means of Intellectual Improvement

There are some to whom it will appear far-fetched to argue for this observance on the ground of intellectual improvement. Such, however, can have paid little attention to one of the great effects of grace. The influence of family worship on mental culture is only a part of the general influence of religion on the mind. True piety improves the understanding. The worship of God is a means of disciplining the faculties. The domestic worship of God is a means of family cultivation, in respect to the intellectual powers.

When we consider that all sanctification is by means of truth, this is no longer wonderful. "The entrance of Thy words giveth light; it giveth understanding unto the simple" (Psalm 119:130). "The fear of the Lord is the beginning of wisdom" (Proverbs 1:7). No man becomes a true Christian without becoming more instructed and more wise.

It has been held by some that the depravity of man, by reason of the fall, does not extend to the intellectual powers; but this is an error against which genuine reformed theology has firmly protested. The change in regeneration is a change of the whole man. There is no aspect under which this renovation is more frequently set forth in Scripture than that of an illumination of the mind (2 Corinth-

ians 4:4–6; Ephesians 1:18, 5:14; Colossians 1:9; Hebrews
10:32; 1 Peter 2:9; 1 John 5:20). Unless I err, this point has
been too much neglected. The very acts and exercises of a
Christian life conduct directly to mental improvement, and
are in themselves an intellectual discipline. And, among
these, family worship has a prominent share.

Family worship includes the reading of the Scriptures;
and this in itself is one of the most valuable instruments of
cultivating the powers. It is a world of knowledge in itself.
The truths which it presents are the greatest and the most
awakening which can be subjected to human attention. It
is the voice of God. He is Light, and in Him is no darkness
at all; the original, uncreated, eternal, causative Light; the
only source of all knowledge in creatures. He is primeval
and essential Truth. Hence the subjects treated in the Bible
are eminently fitted to stimulate and impress the soul. It
treats those things, concurring many of which we could
not even frame an imagination or venture a guess; the
things of eternity before creation and the things of eternity
after judgment; the fall, redemption, and destiny of man.
Surely we need not prove to Christians that the perusal of
the Scriptures is good for the understanding.

By means of family reading, the Bible becomes in a
manner the sole manual of the house. The ancients used to
say, "Take heed of a man of one book," meaning that such
a man, by perpetual repetition and meditation of the same
topics, and perpetually whetting his mind on the same arguments, must become one whom for acumen and use of
his powers it would be dangerous to encounter in argument. Family worship includes in a sort the daily study of
one volume, which thus becomes the domestic textbook.

The history of reformed Christianity would furnish
abundant instances of the discipline and information

which may be attained by means of the Bible alone, especially where proper pains are taken to compare Scripture with Scripture. Here we gladly avail ourselves of the judgment of a learned prelate of the Anglican church. "It is incredible," says the late Bishop Horsley, "to anyone who has not made the experiment, what a proficiency may be made in that knowledge which maketh wise unto salvation, by studying the Scriptures in this manner, without any other commentary or exposition than what the different parts of the sacred volume mutually furnish for each other. Let the most illiterate Christian study them in this manner, and let him never cease to pray for the illumination of that Spirit by which these books were dictated, and the whole compass of abstruse philosophy, and recondite history, shall furnish no argument with which the perverse will of man shall be able to shake this learned Christian's faith" (Horsley's *Nine Sermons*).

There have been Scottish mechanics, husbandmen, and shepherds who have known no book but the Word of God, and who have nevertheless become able theologians and instructed men. Indeed, it may be considered whether the characteristic and proverbial quickness of the Scottish peasantry may not in a great measure be ascribed to this very source. As a triumphant example of the formative influence of the simple Scriptures on even an unlettered mind, we need only mention the immortal name of John Bunyan.

Let it not be thought that, because the Bible is simply heard by the majority of a household, it falls without effect. Hearing is study, and of the most ancient kind. Before copies of the Word of God were multiplied, as in our happy day, it was by the ear, and not by the eye, that its contents were mostly received. When the manner of reading is good, it is still the most impressive method for the ignorant and the young. By such means family worship becomes a household school, and the tuition goes on for a lifetime. All this holds good even when there is not a syllable of comment. But where there are even moderate gifts, there will sometimes be thrown in a word of remark, the explanation of a hard phrase, the reference to a parallel place, the summons to special attention, the seasonable advice, or the warm entreaty. Sometimes, where time is more at command, parts of a useful commentary will be read in connection with the Word. Sometimes portions of evangelical works will be added, and sometimes the catechetical exercise, according to a venerable Presbyterian custom, will find its place by the side of the domestic worship of the Lord's day.

In a word, I cannot think it possible for any family to enjoy, twice every day for all their lives, the privilege of hearing the Scripture read at domestic worship without, by that very means, rising perceptibly and greatly in knowledge and intellectual force.

The reading of the Bible, invaluable as we own it to be, is, however, but a part, and not the most essential part of family worship. It remains, therefore, to consider the influence of devotion. Although the subject has not been as frequently discussed as its importance deserves, I undertake to maintain that prayer itself is an intellectual discipline. No man can pray habitually without thereby gaining control over his thoughts and the cultivation of his faculties.

Nothing is more generally acknowledged by all who have treated the conduct of the understanding than that an indispensable condition of all right thinking and learning is the power of fixing the attention. In nothing is there a greater difference between the civilized man and the savage, between the adult and the infant, between the philosopher and the boor. There is nothing, therefore, which is more earnestly sought in every method of judicious education. This habit of mental concentration is the result of innumerable acts, and is secured by repeatedly summoning the mind to such acts. An exercise which brings the understanding to converse with great objects in a state of interest, under strong motives to be attentive, and with frequent repetition, directly promotes this habit. Such an exercise is prayer.

If prayer were a sheer formality, like the recital of unintelligible *Aves* and *Credos*, the stringing of beads on a rosary or the revolution of the Tartar's praying-machine, it might fail of any such effect. But it is an exercise in which the understanding is immediately and most actively employed. As one of the first hindrances to prayer is felt to be the wandering of the thoughts, so the very first effort of the mind which addresses itself to devotion is the calling in of the thoughts and fixing of the attention.

Every act of prayer directs the mind towards the greatest of all possible objects. This is plainly a posture in which the faculties cannot be dormant. The connection of thought with thought in prayer is a reasonable connection, and so furnishes exercise to the powers. The accompanying play of strong emotions, such as are evolved in acts of supplication and praise, so far from being detrimental, is highly helpful to the intellectual process; for never does the mind make truer progress than when the moral powers are in high exercise.

Let us compare two men of equal capacity and otherwise alike in their circumstances. One of these has passed a lifetime without prayer. The other has, at stated hours, ten thousand times solemnly addressed himself to the worship of God. Is it possible to believe that such a difference in habit can exist without a corresponding difference in intellectual development? Apply this to the domestic ordinance. From the moment of budding thought, all along the way of years, until the last day of life, the household have been gathered, morning and evening, for attendance on the Scriptures and prayer; to contemplate the great God, to meditate on the best books, to mingle in the most sacred emotions. Such an aggregate of influence, even on the intellect, can never be estimated in the present world; but we surely would violate every principle of the mental constitution were we to deny its greatness. And this is an influence, diffused not merely among theologians and scholars, but over the common mind of a country. We all know how little there is among the mass of men that deserves the name of "thought." The minds of the multitudes are diverted by company, dissipated by frivolous pursuits, or worn by daily labor. For such it is greatly useful to be called to a daily exercise which composes the feelings, breaks the worldly thread, opens connections with eternity, and constrains to the thought of God. Such influences are ennobling. Souls cannot yield themselves so unreservedly to the flesh, nor sink so low in the scale of intelligence and morals, with these as without them. It is something gained to have, twice a day, pauses for thought. Texts and principles poured into the most careless, or, I might even say, the most unwilling mind, and prayers uttered even before the undevout, will now and then recur as suggestions, and be owned with saving effect. And what is this but so much additional thought, reflection, and wisdom?

If, as I maintain, family worship tends directly and powerfully to the promotion of piety, we might here rest our proof of its intellectual benefits. All true piety is enlarging and elevating. It spreads its efficacy over the whole soul. It renders its subject necessarily a meditative and serious person. Evangelical doctrine, such as runs through all sound family worship, is connected with chains of high argument and embodies the most systematic truth. Nowhere is this better exemplified than among our Calvinistic forefathers. Beside the loom, or following the plow, they nevertheless pondered those high points which looser systems deem too abstruse for man, but which are revealed in the Word, and are rendered matter of nourishment and exultation to many a man who earns his bread. I have in memory a Scottish working man, a humble dyer in a factory, whose conversation was a feast of intellectual stores. He was not only the dread of infidel socialists in his own circle, but was abundantly able to converse and to argue on even the minuter divisions of theological science; and he was well versed in the annals of the church. Such cases are not rare, and such men are reared among the institutions of family religion.

A clear addition to the annual means of grace, amounting to seven-hundred distinct religious exercises, is an element which we cannot exclude from just calculation. A town, a province, or a country under such influences would be "a field which the Lord hath blessed." It would contain a population mighty in the Scriptures, and trained to masculine thought. Such a land we should pray that ours may be. It would then be "the glory of all lands." These are among the reasons why we desire the observance of family worship to be universal.

6

*The Influence of Family Worship
on Domestic Harmony and Love*

"Behold, how good and how pleasant it is for brethren to dwell together in unity. It is like the precious ointment upon the head, that ran down upon the beard, even Aaron's beard, that went down to the skirts of his garments. As the dew of Hermon, and as the dew that descended upon the mountains of Zion; for there the Lord commanded the blessing, even life forevermore" (Psalm 133).

Family peace is a blessing which cannot be overrated; and I desire to show that it is directly promoted by family worship.

The stated and punctual assembly of a whole household for the service of God has this tendency, if considered merely as a means of bringing the several members together. There are striking differences between families in regard to the simple quality of cohesion. While some are a bare collection of so many particles without mutual attraction, others are consolidated into a unity of love. Many scattering influences are at work. Some of these may be referred to want of system and regularity, some to late hours, some to peculiarities of business, some to fashion, and some to the dissipations of vice. From one or more of these influences we see domestic harmony impaired. Parents and children meet only at their meals, and not

48

even at all of these. The tardy inmates of the house descend in the morning at any hour and at long intervals, and the evening is often spoiled of the charm of home. In such circumstances we are persuaded the links of affection are tarnished, if not worn away.

In proportion as the subjects of mutual obligation live apart, they will cease to care for one another. No customs of society are laudable or safe which tend, in any considerable degree, to separate parents from children and brothers from sisters. It is good to bring together the coals on the domestic hearth. Hence we have always looked with unqualified satisfaction on the New England custom of gathering all the members of a family, however remote, under the paternal roof on the day of annual thanksgiving. There is a sacred virtue in even beholding the face of an aged father and a gentle, beloved mother. On this very principle, the president of one of our colleges, justly celebrated for his influence on young men, was accustomed, when he saw the first tokens of aberration in a boy, to call him to his study and kindly propose to him a simple visit to his parents. We do not wonder that the effect was often magical.

Family worship assembles the household twice every day, and that in a deliberate and solemn manner. No individual is missing. This is the law of the house from childhood to old age. The observance is as stated as the daily meals. Other employments and engagements are made to bow to this, until it becomes the irreversible rule of the little commonwealth. They look upon one another's faces. They exchange the salutations of affection. Now, if ever, kind words and gentle wishes will be breathed; plans for mutual benefit or entertainment will be laid; and the glow will be not the less because they are met to offer the sacrifice of praise. Taken singly, such influences are not to be despised; but they rise to inestimable magnitude, when diffused through all the days of long years, that is, over the entire progress of family life. By those who have enjoyed them they can never be forgotten. Such households stand in open contrast to those where parents and children, in haste and disorder and with many interruptions, snatch their daily bread without so much as a word of thanks or prayer.

Some good results, in respect of harmony, ensue when a household statedly assembles for the common pursuit of any lawful object whatever. Union, and the sentiment of union, are promoted by joint participation, and the effect is appreciable where the gathering is frequent and stated. Though it were only for exercise or recreation, for the practice of music, for an evening perusal of useful books, still there would be a contribution to mutual acquaintance and regard. But how much stronger is the operation of this principle when the avowed object of this meeting is to seek the face of God and invoke His blessing!

There is no way in which we can more surely increase mutual love than by praying for one another. If you would retain warmth of affection for an absent friend, pray for him. If you would live in the regards of another, beseech him to pray for you. If you would conquer enmity in your own soul towards one who has wronged you, pray for him. Dissension or coldness cannot abide between those who bear each other to God's throne in supplication. It is what we meet to do at family worship. Often has the tenderness of a half-dying attachment been renewed and made young again when the parties have found themselves kneeling before the mercyseat. Everything connected with such utterance of mutual good will in the domestic worship tends to foster it, and thus the daily prayers are as the dews of Hermon. The devotions of the household are commonly conducted by the parent; and parental affection often needs such an outlet. The son or daughter might otherwise remain ignorant of the anxieties of the father. There are yearnings which the parent cannot express to man, not even to a child, but which must be poured forth to God, and which have their appropriate channel in the daily prayer. The hearing of such petitions, gushing warm from the heart, and the participation of such emotions cannot but sometimes reach the hitherto obdurate mind, and tend to a strong and reigning affection. Both parent and child, if they are ever touched with genuine love, must experience it when they come together before their God and Savior.

That revelation of divine truth which is perpetually expressed or implied in family worship in Scripture, in psalms, and in prayers enjoins this very peace and affection. The New Testament presents it on every page. The Word of God and prayer are, from day to day, bringing the duty constantly before the conscience. The household which is subjected to this forming influence may be expected, more than others, to be a household of peace.

Some notice must here be taken of a painful but common case. Human depravity sometimes breaks forth in jars and alienations and strifes among members of the same brotherhood, and, alas, even within the sacred limits of a Christian house. Harsh tempers, sour looks, moody silence, moroseness, grudges, bitter words, and alienations mar the beauty of the circle. Hence we find slights, angry rebukes, suspicions, and recriminations. Happy, indeed, is that household over which these black clouds do not sometimes hover. But what means shall we seek to dispel them which is more efficacious than a common devotion? That must be an obstinate ill-will which not only lets the sun go down on its wrath, but carries it to the altar and to the evening sacrifice. It is hard to listen long to the Word of God without hearing the rebuke of all such dispositions. Perhaps the very portion read may say to the unrelenting one, "If thou bring thy gift to the altar, and there rememberest that thy brother hath aught against thee, leave there thy gift before the altar, and go thy way; first be reconciled to thy brother, and then come and offer thy gift" (Matthew 5:23). At all events, the whole spirit of the exercise breathes such an admonition; and it is most difficult to pray with malice on the heart. Forgiveness comes often to us while we are upon our knees.

Suppose even what we are reluctant to suppose, that mutual reproaches, perverse separation, and open quarrel should enter a religious family. To offenders in such a case, the season of prayer must be an hour of keen rebuke. Avowedly, they are bowed down to pray for one another. The hypocrisy and impiety of so doing out of a mind of hatred will stare the sinner in the face, and may bring him to repentance. Reconciliation, begun in the heart during moments of devotion, may lead to the restoration of peace.

Sad as is the thought that even husband and wife may be drawn asunder and may give place to the devil. Shyness, severity, distrust, and unkindness may spring up between those who have vowed to live together as heirs of the grace of life. But it is hard to believe that such persons, if they possess a spark of grace, can come to the posture and the words of prayer, in which they have been united so many times before in happier days, or can feel themselves encircled by their kneeling little ones, without surrendering the selfish spite, and making a faithful effort to crush the head of the viper. Conjugal tenderness, forbearance and love, are guarded by the exercises of family devotions.

Contrast all this with the condition of a domestic circle subject to the same malign influences, but without these checks and this sacred balm, and you will no longer marvel that, where there is no worship, there is room for discord. The stream of unkindly temper runs on. Brooding silence is the best that can be expected. The day closes without reference to God. The griefs of the day are carried over into the morrow. Infant misconceptions and dislikes have full time to grow to stubborn maturity, and all this for want of that religious influence which would be secured by the hour of prayer.

In speaking of family worship as a means of concord, we might dwell on its influence upon absent members of the household. As children grow up, there are few families which do not send forth from their bosom some to distant places. These are not forgotten at the hearth which they have left. Day by day, the venerable father, joined in silent love by the more melting mother, cries to God for him who is afar upon the sea or in foreign lands. These are moments which bring the cherished object full before the mind, and make the absent one present to the heart. Not to say that such prayers are answered—they kindle and maintain the fire of affection. Most unthinking or most base must be the son or daughter who should fail to prize these parental intercessions, or disregard the supplications of the brother or the sister left at home. Often, I am sure, the recollection of the domestic worship comes up before the distant youth on the high seas or in remote wanderings. Often is the secret tear shed over these privileges of his childhood. In the perpetual fire of family worship, he knows he has a remembrancer in his father's house.

When, after years of absence (and, it may be, of sin),
the son revisits the home of his childhood, and when, at
the close of day, the circle draws around the fireside, and
that worship is renewed which he remembers so well, what
a torrent of ancient reminiscence pours into the heart!
Such associations have their influence on even hardened
natures, and they go to prove the blessedness of this familiar institution.

But after all that we may urge, the great and crowning
reason why domestic worship promotes harmony is that it
promotes true religion, and religion is love. Its mission is
peace on earth and goodwill to men. Christianity compacts
the structure and strengthens every wall. It adds a new ce-
ment, and makes the father more a father, the husband
more a husband, the son more a son; so that there is not a
social tie which does not become more strong and endear-
ing by means of grace. If even enemies are reduced to amity
by the gospel, how much greater must be its influence on
the ties of blood and affinity! It consecrates every natural
relation, and exalts human affections by expanding them
into eternity. Its daily lessons, constantly recurring in family worship, bear directly on this point. "Husbands, love
your wives, even as Christ also loved the Church. Let the
wife see that she reverence her husband. Fathers, provoke
not your children to wrath. Children, obey your parents in
all things, for this is well-pleasing unto the Lord. Servants,
be obedient to them that are your masters according to the
flesh, with fear and trembling, in singleness of your heart,
as unto Christ. And ye masters, do the same thing unto
them, forbearing threatening, knowing that your Master
also is in heaven. Love as brethren, be pitiful, be courteous.
Honor all men. Be kindly affectioned one to another, with
brotherly love, in honor preferring one another. Let all

bitterness, and wrath, and anger, and clamor, and evil-speaking, be put away from you, with all malice: and be ye kind one to another, tender-hearted, forgiving one another, even as God for Christ's sake hath forgiven you." Such are the touching accents of the gospel in general, and of this institution in particular, familiarized to every inmate of a Christian house from the earliest infancy. And what the Word of God enjoins, the Spirit of grace produces in the heart, where true religion finds entrance. Under the daily influence of such motives, which drop as the rain and distill as the dew, the youthful heart may be expected, in many cases, to receive the noblest charities of a renewed nature.

Amidst all the imperfections of the Christian state, there have been thousands of families, since the founding of the Church, which have realized this ideal; and what spectacle on earth is more lovely? From the very cradle the infant lips are taught to lisp the name of God, and the soft voices of childhood join in the daily praise. Brothers and sisters, already brought by baptism within the pale of the visible church, grow up with all the additional reasons for mutual attachment which spring from dedication to God. No day passes in which parents and children do not compass God's altars. When the father and mother begin to descend into the autumn of life, they behold their offspring prepared to walk in their steps. There is a church in the house. When death enters, it is to make but a brief separation; and eternity sees the whole family in heaven without exception or omission.

I quote here the Rev. James Hamilton: "The happiest family will not be always so. The most smiling circle will be in tears some day. All that I ask is that you would secure for yourselves and your children a friend in that blessed

Redeemer who will wipe all tears from your faces. Your families may soon be scattered, and familiar voices may cease to echo within your walls. They may go each to his own, and some of them may go far away. Oh, see to it that the God of Bethel goes with them, that they set up an altar even on a distant shore, and sing the Lord's song in that foreign land. They may be taken from this earth altogether and leave you alone. Oh, see to it that as one after another goes, it may be to their Father's house above, and to sing with heavenly voices and a heavenly harp the song which they first learned from you, and which you often sang together here: the song of Moses and the Lamb. And if you are taken, and some of them are left, see to it that you leave them the thankful assurance that you have gone to their Father and your Father, their God and your God. And, in the meanwhile, let your united worship be so frequent and so fervent that when you are taken from their head, the one whose sad office it is to supply your place, as priest of that household shall not be able to select a chapter or a psalm with which your living image and voice are not associated, and in which you, though dead, are not yet speaking to them. And thus my heart's wish for you all is:

> *When soon or late you reach that coast,*
> *O'er life's rough ocean driven;*
> *May you rejoice, no wanderer lost,*
> *A family in heaven.*

7

The Influence of Family Worship on A Household in Affliction

In hours of trial the members of a household gather together, as if by a natural instinct, and the tendency is more marked where the Christian sympathies are active. But it is an unsatisfactory and cheerless assembling when chastisement falls on a house where there is no religion. The countenances, even of friends, mutually reflect despondency. Words of comfort may be uttered, but they are such as cannot reach the depth of suffering; for what but the promise of the gospel can bind up the broken-hearted? There is a hollowness and conscious insufficiency in the language of condolence which ungodly men address to one another under misfortune. There is no reference to God; there are no allusions to heaven, nor applications by prayer to the great Source of comfort.

In contrast with this, consider the case of a sorrowing believer. The very first impulses when he is smitten are to go to his Father in heaven, whom he recognizes as the Disposer of the event, and whom he leans upon for support. It is the universal experience of disciples: when surprised by trial they flee to the throne of grace, as the frightened bird flees to its covert and nest. "Is any afflicted, let him pray." The operation of this principle is observed in the family. A common visitation has reached every member, but only to drive them more near together. They have learned to bear one another's Christian love. They need no prompter to draw them in concert to the place of prayer; all hearts tend in that very direction, and the sentiments of all find expression in the privilege of family prayer.

Among God's people on earth, there are thousands who smart under the daily affliction of poverty. It is still true that God has chosen the poor of this world to be rich in faith and heirs of the kingdom which He has promised to those who love Him. Though we have not seen the righteous forsaken, yet we have often seen him in such straits that the morning could give no promise of the evening's bread. It is a heavy trial for the father to come home to his household at night, with scarcely enough earnings to keep them from being famished, and for him to behold the wife and little ones shivering for lack of fuel and raiment. Yet such fathers and such households there are where, nevertheless, this very evening the Word of God is read and the blessing which makes rich is invoked in the never-forgotten family prayer. And such families are unspeakably distinguished from the poor, if only by this single service. They have a solace which the world does not understand. That father and mother can lie down, resting on promises of relief which have never been disappointed. And those children, from their earliest years, are learning the lesson of dependence on God, and offering the petition, "Give us this day our daily bread," with an accent unknown in the houses of the rich. True piety may be left without worldly goods, but it will not be left without domestic worship.

Sudden losses are accounted great trials, and they sometimes fall on such as have rolled in wealth. From the vicissitudes of trade, the wildness of speculation, the prodigality of wealth, and the growing treachery of associates, it has come to pass that we hear without surprise of instanta-

neous ruin and bankruptcy. Knit together as society is, this
may befall even a righteous man; or unexpected poverty
may come in at some other door. Riches have many wings
with which they fly away as an eagle toward heaven. In
such a case it is not for one of God's children to say, "Ye
have taken away my gods, and what have I more?" (Judges
18:24). Rather he will call together his household and
humbly declare, with one in worse condition, "The Lord
gave, and the Lord hath taken away; blessed be the name of
the Lord" (Job 1:21). A domestic usage which makes this
not only easy, but expected is a means of relief. Here the
father may pour out his soul freely, and here the children
may learn that their parent has a treasure laid up where
thieves do not break through nor steal. If family devotions
have been held precious during the time of prosperity, they
will seem doubly precious now; and it will be delightful to
consider that earthly reverses cannot touch this possession.
The equipage and livery and plate may vanish; the paintings
and gorgeous furniture may fly under the hammer; the li-
brary may be scattered; the very mansion may be forsaken.
Yet in a cottage or a garret within bare cold walls, shunned
by the parasites of other days, the Christian family may rejoice that the daily worship of God is still untouched; and
here, though with tearful eyes, they can still, from the bot-
tom of their hearts, give thanks. There is, to my mind,
something peculiarly sacred in the worship of the house,
perpetuated, unchanged, through every vicissitude of for-
tune.

"I was once told," says Mr. Hamilton, "of a cottage patriarch who was born in those days when Scotland had a
church in almost every house. There was one in his father's
dwelling, and when he pitched a tent for himself he built an
altar. Round that altar a goodly number of olive plants grew

up; but one by one they were either planted out in families of their own or God took them, till he and his old partner found themselves, just as at their outset in life, alone. But their family worship continued as of old. At last his fellow-traveler left him. Still he carried on the worship by himself. So sweet was the memory of it in his father's house, and so pleasant had he found it in his own, that he could not give it up. But as he sat in his silent habitation, morning and evening, his quivering voice was overhead singing the old psalm-tune, reading aloud the chapter, and praying as if others still worshipped by his side."

When evil tidings come to the heathen, they rend their garments, tear out their hair, cast dust and ashes on their heads, and fill the air with lamentation. Ungodly persons in Christian lands, in a like case, do not indeed give way to the same outward demonstrations, but are not the less affected within. It is the property of the true Christian to hear such messages with calmness and resignation. "He shall not be afraid of evil tidings; his heart is fixed, trusting in the Lord" (Psalm 112:7). And when the black seal is broken, and the faces of all who hover around gather paleness, it is true religion which lifts the eyes and says, "The will of the Lord be done." Blessed is the privilege in such an hour of meeting as a smitten, but unforsaken flock at the feet of the heavenly Shepherd and pouring out the soul in supplication.

Sometimes disease makes fearful inroads in the Christian house. There is then a special message to the throne of grace. Happy is the case in which we can go to Christ, saying, "He whom Thou lovest is sick." But we may bring all our afflicted ones to Him, as to the great Physician, pleading with Him by His name, "JEHOVAH-ROPHI" (Exodus 15:26). The daily visits of the medical adviser are

less indispensable than daily resort to the Most High. It is
not safe to lie ill in a prayerless house; but it is better to be a
Lazarus in the midst of true prayers than to be full of health
in a house which knows no worship. In a faithful household, the case of the languishing sufferer is never forgotten
before God; and the prayer of faith still often heals the sick.
The very thought of this is a cordial to the fainting spirit,
especially in those cases where the malady is lingering and
stretches its saddening influence through many years. The
sons of gaiety may look with indifference on the daily exercise of devotion; not so the pining invalid, whose life is a
long disease, who seldom ventures across the threshold, and
who counts the hours until the voice of prayer and praise is
heard again. When disease takes a more threatening form
and life is in danger, we have observed an unusual solemnity steal over even the more careless members of the
household as they obey the summons to evening prayer.
The feeling is natural that, after all, this is the most rational
instrumentality; for God only can help. The ordinary exercise is transformed into a special intercession for one who is
on a bed of peril. Before the morrow that soul may be in
eternity. Can we think with composure of such dangers, or
of the death struggle going on in houses where not one syllable of oral prayer is uttered, not one group of kneeling
supplicants gathered about the death bed? We may surely
be forgiven if we pray, "May I die the death of the righteous, and may my last end be among the prayers of the
righteous." Yet what numbers are even this moment dying
without one word of supplication, and without so much as a
token of Christianity!

There is a sentiment in every true disciple's breast
which makes him glory in the faith of the gospel pre-
eminently in a moment of tribulation. Now, he feels, is the

juncture in which to show that the confidence in God is unshaken. Hence the quiet and seemly attendance of a Christian household on divine offices, even amidst extreme trials, is strongly opposed to the heathenish confusion of a prayerless family.

Every house must, sooner or later, become a house of mourning. The blessedness of worshipping God in our family capacity is never more evinced than when death has struck his blow. Though we do not pray for the dead, we feel within us an impulse to kneel and pray beside the dead. When the corpse is still in the house, family worship has a singular awe. A link has been broken. A voice is missed from the harmony. A shadowy form that, as long as strength endured, lingered about these places of prayer, has at length ceased to appear. "One is not" (Genesis 42:13). Amidst such unavoidable reflections, the common resort to the throne of grace becomes peculiarly tender and awful. The elevations of prayer and praise befit the soul which has felt a mighty grief, and which sickens at the presentation of minor and earthly considerations. I have seen the earthy considerations. I have seen the heart-broken widow led in to the accustomed place of prayer, shrinking to hear a stranger's voice in the place of her husband's, yet calmed and buoyed up by the fellowship of devotion. Oh, how many could rise and testify that in seasons of deep affliction they have found unutterable solace not only in prayer in general, but in domestic prayer in particular! Wounded hearts need fellowship even in their devotions, and feel their griefs assuaged when others whom they love gather around them in the use of words which make their sorrows the sorrows of all. Such devotions soften and hallow grief, and make the sorrows of a Christian house altogether different from those of the world. To enter such a circle is good. There we are taught that "it is better to go to the house of mourning than to go to the house of feasting" (Ecclesiastes 7:2). Tears will no doubt gush freely and interrupt the service where sudden bereavement has occurred; but the whole influence of the devotion, even on the chief sufferers, has been uniformly observed to be consolatory in no common degree. There are other afflictions, however, besides the loss of property, health, or friends, sometimes less tolerable, more poignant than these. When such tempests break over a house, where can they resort but to God in prayer? If they have already instituted this daily exercise, they need no new arrangements; their access is direct to the heart of their Father. Let them as a family, bowing before Him, unbosom themselves of that burden which, perhaps, they have no freedom to tell to a fellow-man. It is good to draw near to God with peculiar sorrows.

There are houses in our world of suffering where the wonderful dealing of Providence presses with long-continued chastisement; sorrows which abide for years, and from which nothing promises an outlet but death, which brings with it the cure of all evils to the righteous and the answer of all prayers. There are thorns in the flesh which God does not see fit to extract; domestic crosses, constitutional infirmities, vexations left like the Canaanites in the land, incurable pains and diseases. In these it is a blessed thing to pray, and to pray in fellowship. To these, daily worship is a morning and an evening balm as indispensable as the "necessary food." Remove this agency and you strike out the light of the dwelling. Aged and solitary persons, and victims of mental depression, crave the social flow of affection which is afforded by family worship. Having ceased to look for the pity of the world, they need all the more those communications which are made in the hour of prayer, and here they sometimes learn to "glory in tribulation also." Forlorn, indeed, are such sufferers in prayerless households. It is no common trial for a solitary believer to spend a lifetime in a family where there is no other voice to cry to God. And blessed is that institution, handed down to us from our forefathers, by means of which a refreshing stream is daily conducted through the habitation.

A single mourner is, perhaps, found in a household, a stricken deer that left the herd, "long since, with many an arrow deep infixed." Common sympathy does not reach such a case; but it is reached by devotion. Secret balsams of Christian love often distill on the wounded heart in the season of domestic worship, though not a syllable is uttered which, by rude allusion, could shock the sensitive mind. Prayers offered in the presence of such a one take a form which soothes, instructs, and elevates. There is society in worship even for the most secluded mourner. The daily sanctuary of the household would be worth all it could ever cost if it did no more than minister to this diseased mind. In a long night of pilgrimage, without the lights of earthly hope, prayer opens views of the better country; for we are never nearer to heaven than when we are upon our knees.

But reverting to those afflictions which are felt by a whole family, we may observe that they offer remarkable occasions for experiencing the benefits of household devotion. The soul is mollified by grief; every word spoken at such times sinks deeply. Supposing the head of the family to be suitably exercised, his experience will diffuse itself to the members. The youngest and the most worldly will be called to join in lively expressions, which may awaken them to reflection, and lead them to turn the dispensations of Providence to spiritual account. The profound humiliation of a heart-stricken father, his penitent confessions of sin, his unreserved submission to the stroke of God's hand, his moving entreaties for deliverance, comfort, and grace, and his irrepressible intercessions with God for his unconverted children are appeals more likely to go to the heart of the impenitent in a time of sorrow than all the amplifications of eloquence. And as afflictions are sure to be remembered, this means will cause them to be remembered as associated with the most affecting truths of religion.

Let us not forget that God does not always chide, neither does He keep His anger forever. Though weeping may endure for a night, joy comes in the morning. Prayers are answered. They cry unto the Lord in their trouble, and He delivers them out of their distresses. Then comes the time for thanksgiving: to praise the Lord for His goodness, and for His wonderful works to the children of men. A whole family engaged in rendering thanks is a delightful spectacle. The place to behold it is the chamber of family prayer. The psalms and praises of such a service are better than mountains of sacrifice. The house from which they ascend is a Bethel. Where God's worship has been maintained for years, one may look back upon the successive seasons of deliverance and gratitude, and see each one marked with its separate Ebenezer. Can religious professors willingly spend their lives in the reception of divine benefits, and yet withhold from themselves and their children the appropriate solemnity for such tribute of thanksgiving! Shame on the degeneracy of our day, which has made household irreligion a common thing, even within the pale of the visible Church!

We have enlarged upon the topic of affliction as connected with family worship because afflictions are the common lot of all, and because they remarkably show the value of this institution. We know no sight more touching

than that of a Christian family, under some humbling,
piercing dispensation, all gathered in the accustomed place
of prayer, like fearful birds overtaken by a storm, and seeking the Lord God of Israel, under whose wings they come
to trust (Ruth 2:12). Rising from prayer and separating for
the night, they find their agitations calmed by the presence
of the Comforter, and can say with hope, "O Lord, be gracious unto us; we have waited for Thee: be Thou their arm
every morning, our salvation also in the time of trouble"
(Isaiah 33:2). The ungodly are not so. These softening and
consoling influences are unknown to them. Their griefs are
sullen. No fellowship in waiting upon God lifts them above
the cold, barren prospect of earthly consolations. Their
dwellings are dark and wintry, in respect to any stated service of God. And, alas, they are imitated by many in the
Church who endure the stokes of chastisement again and
again, and even sustain the arrows of death, without having
ever known what it was to come together as a family for
prayer. Would it be credited by a Jew, a Mohammedan, or
a heathen, that men who profess the religion of Jesus, and
sit down at His table, die and are carried out to burial from
houses in which their voices have never been heard in
prayer?

8

The Influence of Family Worship on Visitors, Guests, and Neighbors

As "none of us liveth to himself, and no man dieth to himself," it is right and seemly that this principle of devotion to the Lord should be impressed on the domestic organization. The Christian household is not for itself; by grace it may be as a city set on a hill. Family worship is a means of carrying out this influence.

Good and evil are constantly and rapidly propagated from house to house. What we denominate public opinion and public character are very much dependent on this agency, which is no less certain than the silent but mighty transmission of the electric fluid in the material world. The dialect of towns and provinces is thus originated and fixed; modes of dress, furniture, and living are carried from circle to circle; extravagance and vice circulate by the same channels, as do likewise political opinions, and even religious sentiments. Such are the action and reaction between man and man, that we never go into a neighbor's house, or receive a neighbor into our own, without giving or receiving some imperceptible impression; and by the sum of these are our character and manners formed.

Families differ very widely with respect to their freedom of intercourse. While some are shut up within themselves, others keep open doors and are frequented by numbers of visitors and guests. When the friend whom we cherish is under our roof, he should be made to discern the reigning principle of the place. In a dwelling where there is no worship, he may be pardoned if he says, "Surely the fear of God is not in this place" (Genesis 20:11). But in a religious household, even the casual visitor must sometimes be made sensible that there is a perpetual reference to another world. Suppose him to be under the Christian roof at the appointed hour of prayer. It is well in every such case if the service is not omitted or postponed. He may be a stranger to such solemnities. He may be even careless or profane. Yet when he sees the whole family gathered with stillness and decorum, when he hears the Word of God read, joins in the psalm of praise, and kneels with the rest in an act of worship, it will be no marvel if he is drawn to some new and serious reflection. The impression may be greater than we suppose from the very influence of novelty. These acts of divine service will have a tendency to show him that here, at least, is a circle in which God is continually recognized. If he is a householder himself, he will necessarily be led to contrast with this the condition of his own domestic affairs; and if he is a professing Christian, living in neglect of this duty, he will doubtless experience a pang of conscience. Example is powerful. He may see his way more clear to make his own habitation a house of prayer.

"Some years ago," says Mr. Hamilton of London, "an Irish wanderer, his wife, and his sister, asked a night's shelter in the cabin of a pious schoolmaster. With the characteristic hospitality of his nation, the schoolmaster made them welcome. It was the hour for evening worship, and when the strangers were seated he began by reading slowly and solemnly the second chapter of the epistle to the Ephesians. The young man sat astonished. The expressions 'dead in trespasses and sins,' 'children of wrath,' and 'walking after the course of this world,' were new to him. He sought an explanation. He was told that this is God's account of the state of man by nature. He felt that it was exactly his own state: 'In this way I have walked from my childhood. In the service of the god of this world I have come to your house.' He was on the way to a fair, where he intended to pass a quantity of counterfeit money. But God's Word had found him out. He produced his store of coin, begged his host to cast it into the fire, and asked anxiously if he could not obtain the Word of God for himself. His request was complied with, and next morning, with the new treasure, the party who had now no errand to the fair returned to his own home. Perhaps by this time the pious schoolmaster has met his guest within the gates of the city, outside of which are thieves, and whatsoever makes a lie. But I cannot enumerate all the conversions which have occurred at the Church in the house."

"A few years ago," says the same writer, "an English gentleman visited America, and spent some days with a pious friend. He was a man of talent and accomplishments, but an infidel. Four years afterwards he returned to the same house a Christian. They wondered at the change, but little suspected when and where it had originated. He told them that when he was present at their family worship, on the first evening of his former visit, and when after the chapter was read, they all knelt down to pray, the recollection of such scenes in his father's house long years ago rushed on his memory so that he did not hear a single word. But the occurrence made him think, and his thoughtfulness ended in his leaving the howling wilderness of infidelity and finding a quiet rest in the salvation wrought out by Jesus Christ."

By this pleasing incident I am led to observe that the

influence of family worship is peculiarly great upon guests who abide for some days or weeks in a Christian house, even if they have been brought up at home without such privileges. All that has just been pointed out here operates more freely and for a longer time. The beauty of holiness and the pleasantness of the ways of God are silently brought before their contemplations. I could name instances in which such a sojourn in a pious family has made deep impressions on worldly minds in favor of evangelical religion. This ought surely to rest on the thoughts of Christian householders in the way of duty. We are, perhaps, ready enough to make our guests welcome, to provide for their lodging and refreshment, to show them the wonders of our environs, and to invite friends for their entertainment; but, besides this, we owe a duty to their souls. It ought not for a moment to be thought possible that a dear friend or relative should stay weeks, or even days, in our house without receiving some spiritual advantage. How often have the visits of careless young persons to godly families been made instrumental of their salvation. Among the means tending in this direction, I know of none more fruitful than that which forms the subject of this volume.

But I must by no means narrow down the efficacy of daily worship to that which takes place within a particular house. The whole neighborhood feels the influence. Let us not undervalue the power of Christianity. No single believer can abide long in a place without making it in some degree better; the true leaven will work; the true light will shine. Nor can any consistent God-fearing household fail of diffusing a hallowed force in every direction. Bad influences fly thus; why shall not good ones? It is true from the depravity of our nature that men follow evil rather than good; but it is also true, blessed be God, that divine grace uses the very same channels of connection for the conveyance of truth and holiness. Suppose only a single pious family, observing the worship of God, without shame or concealment, in the midst of a wicked society. Their peculiar ways, and this service in particular, will attract notice and beget remark. The visitor, or the passer-by, will hear the voice of praise or prayer. The observation will be natural: That house is a house of prayer, and God is honored in that house. Neighbors will learn that here is a man who arranges all his business and fixes all his hours with reference to the daily household devotion, which nothing is allowed to interrupt. There are occasions in which this peculiarity of the dwelling is brought into full light. In cases of sudden illness, calamity, or soul trouble, everyone will know where to go for a praying man to kneel by the bed of death, or to speak peace to the troubled conscience. Where such households are multiplied in any town or neighborhood by means of counsel and example, there is a mighty increase given to the expansive Christian principle, such as often changes the whole face of society. How earnestly ought we to pray that this particular means of social and national improvement may receive an immediate extension throughout our beloved land; and that unfaithful professors, living in neglect of this plain duty, may awake to repentance and reformation! What a change might we expect soon to see in regions where now the feeble piety which exists is like a half-expiring taper which scarcely reaches beyond its little home-circle!

I am under the humbling impression that this is one of the points in regard to which, with all our boast of superior privileges, we have not improved on the example of our pious forefathers. Among the Presbyterians of Scotland, and the English Nonconformists of the seventeenth century, there was probably a far smaller proportion of Christian professors living in prayerless houses than among ourselves. The performance of this duty was made a matter of special investigation by pastors and elders, and even by superior judicatories of the church. And the effect was a diffusion of piety, more unobtrusive perhaps, but not less rapid, and certainly not less sound, than that which, in our day, we are fond of seeking by periodical excitements and doubtful measures. The sacred treasure of one house became the portion of many, and whole communities caught the fire which may have been enkindled in a corner. Such was the case in the town of Kidderminster, which was blessed with the labors of that eminent servant of God, Richard Baxter; and his testimony, however familiar, is too valuable to be omitted in this place.

"On the Lord's day, "says Mr. Baxter, "there was no disorder to be seen in the streets, but you might hear a hundred families singing psalms and repeating sermons as you passed through. When I came there first, there was about one family in a street that worshipped God and called on His name; and when I came away, there were streets where there was not above one family in the side of a street that did not so, and that did not, by professing serious godliness, give us some hopes of their sincerity; and those families which were the worst, being inns and alehouses, usually some persons in each did seem to be religious. Some of the poor men did competently understand the body of divinity, and were able to judge difficult controversies. Some of them were so able in prayer that very few ministers did match them in order and fullness and apt expressions, and holy oratory with fervency. Many of them were able to pray very laudably with their minds, and the innocence of their lives was much more laudable than their parts."

It may sometimes be the case that a man of humble station and defective culture of mind may be called upon to perform this duty in the presence of guests or strangers, whom he regards as much superior to himself; and this will doubtless be a trial to his faith. But let him not shrink from the service of God. In a majority of instances, those very persons will go away with a higher estimate of his character for this very act of duty. Each of us should remember the words of David when he said, "I will speak of Thy testimonies also before kings, and will not be ashamed" (Psalm 119:46). When George IV was in Ireland, as we find recorded by the Rev. Dr. Sprague, he told Lord Roden that, on a particular morning, he would breakfast with him. He accordingly came, bringing with him two or three of the nobility, and happened to arrive just as his lordship and family were assembled for domestic worship. Lord Roden, being informed that his royal guest had arrived, went to the door, and, with every token of respect, conducted him into the house. Then, turning to the king, he said, "Your Majesty will not doubt that I feel highly honored by this visit; but there is a duty which I have not yet discharged this morning, which I owe to the King of kings—that of performing domestic worship; and your Majesty will be kind enough to excuse me while I retire with my household and attend to it." "Certainly," replied the king, "but I am going with you." And he immediately rose and followed him into the hall where the family were assembled; and, taking his seat in an old arm-chair, the king remained during the family devotion.

In reading accounts of the persecuted non-conformists, it is remarkable how often we find that they were arrested by pursuivants and other officers at the time of family worship. This was an hour when they were sure to be taken to-

gether. Besides, at a time when the public gifts of Christ's
ministers were restrained by the Act of Uniformity, it was
not unusual for neighbors to come in at the season of domestic prayer; and thus the household assembly would often become an unlawful conventicle. Even in our own day,
ministers of the gospel, and other pious persons, have
opened their doors to neighbors who thirsted for truth and
devotion; and in this way the religion of the family may extend itself with blessings to the vicinity. The household
prayer-meeting cannot have a more auspicious origin. Oh,
when will we behold the day when every professing Christian in our Church shall be duly awakened to the power of
the instrumentality which is lodged in his hands!

9

The Influence of Family Worship in Perpetuating Sound Doctrine

Those for whom these pages are chiefly intended are in nothing more fully agreed than in this, that every portion of divine truth is precious, and that every deviation, however small, from the faith once delivered to the saints is most earnestly to be deprecated. Hence unusual care was taken by our pious forefathers, in so framing compendious forms of doctrine, and so inculcating them upon the infant mind, and so exacting adherence to them from church-officers, as might best preclude departures from the original, covenanted testimony. This has not been unobserved by our adversaries, and we are familiar as a church with the charge of being stiff, opposed to innovations, and tenacious of the traditions of the elders.

Though no human guards can maintain sound doctrine, we must, nevertheless, avail ourselves of every lawful means. There is a constant tendency to deflect from the line of true direction. It arises from the depraved nature and has manifested itself in every successive age, from that of the apostles downwards. Hence the necessity for God's frequent and gracious interposition in the way of reformation and revival. Thus the great work which was wrought by the instrumentality of Luther was a clearing away of wood, hay, and stubble, errors and abuses which had been built on the primitive foundation. The early Lutheran church was, comparatively, pure. But even before the death of that mighty man of God, tares began to be visible among the wheat; and those who succeeded him allowed serious errors to creep in, especially in regard to the decrees of God. In the eighteenth century this dereliction of the old faith became more and more striking until, in the present day, not only Arminian-ism and Pelagianism, but Arianism, Sabellian-ism, Socinianism, and that form of atheism which is called "Pantheism," are known to prevail among preachers and professors. And though we rejoice in manifest tokens that God is arising to have mercy on that land, we have still to lament the wide departures of multitudes from the truth. In Geneva, the very place of Calvin's teaching, and of his death, the growth of heresy has been so rapid that until the late gracious awakenings which have raised up witnesses for the doctrines of the gospel, the whole body of the ministry had gone astray. The case of Boston and of Harvard College is well known to all our readers. In England, a large number of the churches called Presbyterian have become Unitarian. The piety of ancestors conveys no hereditary blessing to their children. Nor do we believe it to be the purpose of God to connect perpetuity of faith with any form of external service, however excellent. Yet we are deeply persuaded that among the means which He is pleased to use for this end, one of the most prominent is family worship. If anything has been attained by our investigations thus far, it has been shown that family worship is promotive of piety. It is in this very way that it is promotive of sound-ness in the faith. Truth and holiness act and react on one another. The first instrumentality is doubtless that of the truth by which, in the hand of the Spirit, the work of sanctification is effected. But no less undeniable is that further influence by which the graces of the soul foster the doctrines of the Word. All defection from the faith begins in decay of piety. Sound doctrine is a plant that will not flourish in a soil which has lost the warmth of gracious affection. There may be scriptural creeds in the very words of the venerable reformers—such are the confessions of Germany, Holland, and the Swiss churches—but the body of the people, and especially the clergy, will go off into the most destructive errors. There was a period of "dead orthodoxy," as it was called in Germany, which preceded the grand apostasy. For a time there was fiery contention for the symbols, resulting in the unrelenting persecution of such men as Spencer, Francke, and Canstein; but shortly the door was opened for the eruption of a rationalistic deism. Decay of vital godliness leads rapidly to heterodox teaching. Times of outward prosperity are seized by the adversary for carrying on this disastrous work. Wealth flows into the church, and Christian professors, forgetting their vocation as a "peculiar people," emulate the world in their expenditure, their equipage, and their entertainments. The question which is common among us, as to the lawfulness of certain frivolous amusements, is a question which could not be so much as agitated in a flourishing and spiritual church. No man can think of it as mooted among the apostles or early martyrs, among the reformers or convenanters. But at a certain stage in the declension we find members of the church opening their houses for the midnight dance, then going freely to the theater and to games of hazard, and finally making shipwreck of the faith. As piety decays, there is great tenderness for error, and great latitude in the exposition of doctrine. A spurious charity forbids every word of harshness towards even gross error. Indifference is the mother of heresy, as we may read in the annals of Wittenberg, Geneva, and Cambridge; and both have their descent from worldliness in the church. Whatever, therefore, promotes piety, in the same degree promotes the belief of truth.

Family worship is one of those observances which it is difficult to maintain for any length of time without at least some sentiment of reverence for evangelical truth. More public and ceremonious ordinances may continue to be rendered necessary and decorous by the customs of society; but the prayer of the household is apt to fall into disquietude when the spirit in which it originated has altogether fled.

It is worthy of observation that there is something in the very temper engendered by family worship which favors persistence in the faith. It is a temper of mingled love and veneration. We entertain no respect for that youthful independence which exhibits itself in the division of Christian households, and in the going off of sons and daughters to this or that religious community, while, perhaps, the aged pair are left to totter on, unsupported, to the ancient church. Our estimate of a young man does not rise when he takes pride in showing that he does not care what may have been the opinion of his father. Such is not the disposition which is nurtured by the daily worship of a godly house. The body of associations which is formed by repeatedly engaging for long years in acts of common devotion with honored parents is very strong and lasting, and manifestly leads, unless there are powerful and conscientious reasons on the other part, to the maintenance of the tenets which those parents loved. The recollection of a departed father or mother, as employed in the patriarchal conduct of domestic worship, has often, I doubt not, been an operative bond to restrain the wayward youth from false teachings. And though some may be disposed, without ceremony, to tear asunder and cast away such cords as hostile to independence of thought, I have always observed them to be strongest in the most ingenuous and noble natures. Family religion is therefore eminently conservative, and stands among the barriers on which we most rely against an inundation of errors.

But there is something more than an appeal to blind affection in the power of domestic piety to perpetuate sound doctrine. Family worship, from its very nature, keeps the mind attentive to truth and familiar with its smallest ramifications. The way in which great truths fall into discredit, be it observed, is not by being refuted, but by being kept out of view. Hence you may hear even a whole series of Socinian discourses, from a smooth, wily teacher without a single word against the Trinity or the way of salvation. All is negative; but the result, as in the churches of Boston, is positive and ruinous heresy. Who can fail to perceive the advantage of a daily exercise which holds before the minds of youth, in a natural and unobtrusive, yet satisfactory manner, the leading doctrines of religion?

Where the Scriptures are fully and statedly read in a household day by day, there is the greatest possible safeguard against error. We desire no other orthodoxy than that which is contained in this Rule of Faith. We leave it to Rome to be afraid of the volume. Our venerated formulas of faith were drawn up by men who, though for the most part educated under other influences, derived their tenets from the naked Word. By this we are ready to abide; and we maintain with earnestness that the best of all methods for preventing latitudinarian declension is a perpetual inculcation of the Scriptures, such as is continually taking place in family worship. Though there may be some marked exceptions in times of controversy, and among disputants, it is a general truth that errorists are seldom great textuaries. Heterodoxy becomes weary of a record which must be garbled and tortured before it can speak the new language; while, on the other hand, we venture the assertion that no race of men ever existed to whom the very words of Scripture have been so familiar as those who, among our ancestors, have professed the strictest doctrines of the Reformation. A Christian family is brought daily to the fountain of all truth.

Prayer itself inculcates truth. All acceptable prayer is founded on distinct views of doctrine. The posture of the soul in prayer, moreover, is favorable to the reception of those very doctrines which are commonly the first ones to be impugned. Hence it is a trite and true saying that the errorists are more sound in their prayers than in their preaching. This is natural. One of the most common deviations into error regards human ability to keep God's law. But he who is upon his knees will falter before he can address the Almighty with any boast of such ability. Many, I am sure, have bewailed their original depravity, and confessed their natural corruption in prayer who have denied it in books and sermons; and many, I believe, have pleaded the righteousness of Christ imputed to the believing soul as their only meritorious ground of justification who have stoutly denied the possibility of such an imputation. These remarks are made for the purpose of showing that prayer itself is a vehicle for the conveyance of sound doctrine, and that he who, in a Christian house, listens from year to year to the voice of humble, ardent supplication, especially from parental lips, and who, by the very nature of the exercise, is called to make the sentiments his own, is already in a school of theology whose instructions tend to maintain his adherence to the faith of his church.

In old Presbyterian families, it has been a usage to connect the catechetical instruction of children and servants with the domestic worship of the Lord's day evening. It is a beautiful and blessed remnant of Reformation customs, and we have gained nothing by allowing it in any degree to pass away. There is a propriety in having at least one hour of the week in which the Christian parent may take the place of a solemn instructor in divine things, and there is seemliness in connecting these lessons with the season of devotion. There have never been better theologians, nor have there been any more disposed to abide by what they had learned, than those catechumens of the Scottish Sabbath evening. Professors, and even ministers, bearing the Presbyterian name have been known not merely to disuse our venerable catechism, but to sneer at it. Such are the families, the sons of which we shall see, without surprise, flying to other communions, and looking down with contempt on the faith of their fathers.

In the first chapter of this work, I found occasion to lament the decay of family worship in the original seats of the Reformation, and I have now observed the decay of sound doctrine in the same countries. The former neglect may be fairly considered as one of the causes which have wrought the present evils in the Protestant churches of the continent. It is remarkable that where family worship and the due observance of the Sabbath have fallen into disuse, error and worldliness prevail; and it is equally remarkable that one of the prominent symptoms of recovery, wherever the gospel resumes its power, is a return to these ordinances. For I would not be understood as charging upon the whole body of believers on the European continent a disregard of household devotion. In cases where men have been brought to the true light from rationalism and neology, they have exhibited the family likeness which prevails in all "the household of faith." We have been struck with this in the biography of Sybel, a lovely German preacher, who was signally blessed in the training of youth, and whose domestic life is worthy of universal imitation.

"Sybel's domestic life," says a friend, "was very orderly and methodical. He arose very early, between three and four o'clock, awakened his scholars, and, in the same room with them, worked hard till about seven. Then he called the whole family together, and they sang, with the accompaniment of a piano-forte, a few verses from the hymnbook. Sybel read a short portion of Scripture, making a brief application to our necessities, always in a very devout and hearty manner, yet very simple, so that even children and servants could understand. He then prayed, making a similar reference to what was read, and to domestic circumstances, and closed with a short singing. Then followed breakfast, which we took in common, after which he went with the boys to school, where he remained till twelve. At noon he offered a short extemporaneous prayer. In the afternoon, the time was in like manner devoted to his calling. On holidays, there was a longer walk than usual. He was fond of taking some of the boys with him on these occasions, and had a faculty of instructing them by means of plays, songs, and conversation. The day was closed with divine service, like that of the morning" (Arnold August Sybel. *Nach Seinem Leben und Wirken Von Dr. F. Liebetrut.* Berlin:1841).

Now that which affects us in the history of this blessed young man is the fact, that his attachment to these pious observances of the household advanced at equal pace with his progress in evangelical truth.

10

The Influence of Family Worship on the Church

In a certain sense, all the advantages of family worship which are indicated in this volume may be said to redound to the good of the Church; but this is true also of influences which are more special and immediate.

Whatever may be the reflex and incidental consequences of prayer are second to its grand consequence: its answer in heaven. "For everyone that asketh, receiveth; and he that seeketh, findeth; and to him that knocketh, it shall be opened" (Matthew 7:8). The primary advantage of family prayer to the church is that it is answered. It is no small thing for any congregation to have daily cries for God's blessing on it ascending from a hundred firesides. What a spring of refreshment to a pastor! The family devotions of praying Kidderminster, no doubt, made Baxter a better minister and a happier man; and it is possible that we are reaping the fruits of them in his *The Saints' Everlasting Rest* and *Dying Thoughts*. We have all heard of the preacher who told his flock that he had "lost his prayer book," meaning their prayers; as also that good quaint saying of the last age, "A praying people makes a preaching minister." Such aid has been well compared to that of Aaron and Hur (Exodus 17:12). Faithful and affectionate Christians never fail to remember their spiritual guide in their household supplications. Though we cannot trace the connection, such prayers are often answered in the house of God. Amidst the peculiar trials and discouragements of a laborious pastor, it is one of his chief restoratives to know that he is thought of by the family groups of worship in every part of his parish. This stimulates him to give all possible diffusion to the observance; and as his praying household increases, the strength of his arm is increased of God. Every considerate minister will rejoice in stated service of so much simplicity, and susceptible of so easy enlargement, for keeping him and his wants and his sacred work everyday before some portion, if not the whole, of his charge.

But the pastor is not the church, though he is an important member of it, and though his spiritual prosperity is an index of the prosperity of the church. Within the parish bounds there are other objects to be prayed for, and these cannot but arise before the praying household. Let us not be thought to give them undue prominence when among these we specify the poor and the afflicted. God has chosen them for separate regard. "He that honoreth Him hath mercy on the poor" (Proverbs 14:31). It is very remarkable that when Peter, James, and John came to an agreement with Paul and Barnabas about their respective fields of labor, the one additional point which had a distinct memorandum was, in the language of Paul, "only they would that we should remember the poor; the same which I also was forward to do" (Galatians 2:10). The indigent members of a church are, in a special manner, committed to the love and prayers of Christian families who, while they have enough and to spare, will perhaps cause their prayers and their alms together to "come up for a memorial before God" (Acts 10:4). There are other trials of the fellow-heirs which are to be borne in mind. Such is the unity of the catholic body that we ought, at some seasons, to remember before God every brother and sister in Christ Jesus throughout all the earth. It is a delightful part of fraternal intercession which brings to our hearts more sensibly than anything else can do the oneness of the body of Christ. There are scattered cases in different parts of the world of brethren who are so insulated, and so remote from any help, that they would have none to pray for them unless this spirit of expansive love prevailed in the Church. Among the revelations of the last day, we shall possibly discover that some of the richest blessings we ever received have descended on us in answer to the prayers of brethren whose faces we shall first behold on that day.

If there is any case of extraordinary affliction in a particular church, it will be brought to remembrance in the hour of family prayer. Such references touch the heart. They educate youthful sensibility, and train up the Christian child to "rejoice with them that do rejoice, and weep with them that weep" (Romans 12:15).

Intercessory prayer is a part of devotion which is much neglected. The late, excellent William Romaine has a treatise on this subject which deserves perusal—his own practice being most exemplary. He kept a list of friends, ministers, afflicted persons, and others whom by name he made the subjects of special intercession. At first he devoted a single afternoon each week to this work of love; but his catalogue increased so much that he was constrained to devote to it an additional evening. In our letters and our partings we are accustomed, often too formally, to ask the prayers of our friends. Such requests are apt to be forgotten. Family worship brings them to mind. Here we can relieve beloved brethren whom we may be unable to help in any other way. And what can be more beautiful than all the members of a church daily praying for one another! The judgment day will bring to light unnumbered benefits conferred in answer to the requests of devout families.

Besides the direct consequences of family prayer in blessings on the church, there are others which must not be overlooked. Not to repeat that the whole tone of piety in a congregation is elevated by household devotion, the interests of the religious community, as such, are kept continually before the mind. Those who pray for a blessing on the Word will be most apt to expect a blessing, most ready to mourn over barren ordinances, most earnest in longing for revival, most compassionate to the souls of impenitent hearers, and most active in admonition and other efforts for the saving of souls. Family prayer is prayer for more than the family; it is prayer for the Church. Thus it seconds the preaching, and cultivates the spirit of love for the whole society. Now that the ancient Puritan usage of repeating in the house the sermon which was heard in the church has fallen into neglect, it is useful to have such prayers offered on the Lord's day evening as may keep up the impression of divine ordinances. On the eve of sacramental services, the daily request of many families for the special presence of Christ is a means of edification to all concerned. In times of awakening, when multitudes are under the pangs of conviction for sin, there is unspeakable preciousness in a daily exercise which presents their case before God, and which tends to diffuse the healthful influence on every side.

All these incidental advantages derived by the Church from family worship may be referred to a single principle: the interests of the body are brought home to the house. "Now are they many members, yet but one body" (1 Corinthians 12:20). The views of the humble, private Christian are enlarged to take in, first, the particular church of which he is a member, and then the whole assemblage of Christ's people. Surely this is no unimportant contribution to catholic unity.

We live in an age when, through divine grace, evangelical Christians all over the earth are awakened to a new zeal for the propagation of the gospel, and for general charity, by means of associated effort. Towards this grand result millions of gold and silver are bestowed; but no gift of the church is equal to her prayers. It is not enough that these enterprises should have a place in the sanctuary; they must have a place at the fireside. As the spirit of missions and the desire for Christ's appearing increase among us, a change will be recognized in our family devotions. The diffusion of God's Word will form a theme of daily supplication. The missionary, the Sabbath-school teacher, and the agent of public benevolence will be solemnly and affectionately commended to God by praying households. Now this cannot be continued for any length of time without a manifest influence on all who are thus employed. The most experienced of the circle will find their public spirit, their philanthropy, and their zeal for Christ's house augmented by this repeated utterance of benevolent desires. The children, youth, and sojourners of the house will learn to view these works of charity as an essential part of religion, never to be out of sight even for so much as a day. No agency will do more to extend and endear as universal the participation of all our church members in the great aggressive work of the Church. A due application of these truths to the prayers of our families would put an end to those mortifying and fearful revelations made from time to time by whole congregations, and even whole presbyteries, which contribute nothing to the spread of the gospel in foreign lands. Prayer would lead to action, and new energy would be infused into our missions (foreign and domestic), our education of pious youth, and our circulation of Christian books through the length and breadth of the land. It is respectfully suggested that pastors and elders may conduce to this end by timely counsels as to the mode of conducting family prayer, and by their own example, when called upon to lead in the prayers of a household. The people at large need to be encouraged to enlarge their petitions for these great objects, and to bring them constantly within the circle of their household devotions.

I have reserved for this place a point which appears to me to be second to no other in its bearing on this branch of our subject; I mean, family prayer for the outpouring of the Holy Spirit on the church. The duty and privilege of such prayer in general are acknowledged by every pious heart. I desire to call attention to the necessity of such prayer as a part of daily household worship. A church is already in a state of revival when all its praying families are thus engaged in sincerity. But in the coldest times, those who fear the Lord should make conscience of bearing this matter on their hearts before God amidst their families. Immense power is thus added to the public ministry of the Word. It is lamentable that so many live as if the whole weight of responsibility was with the preacher, and as if they had no sort of concern in the success of his work. Periods of great awakening, ever since the day of Pentecost, have been commonly preceded by united and earnest prayer for this particular blessing on the part of "the multitude of them that believed." That professing Christian who truly longs for such an awakening as shall bring into the church his children, his neighbors, and all that are afar off, can in no way more directly contribute towards the blessed result than by deliberately and uninterruptedly making it enter into the prayers in which he leads his household. Where this is forgotten, it is no marvel if religion declines, and if the unconverted members of the family draw the natural conclusion that, after all, their impenitent condition is an evil too unimportant to be presented before God.

Why should there not be a union of families in such prayers by an agreement, one day in the week, to regard this with especial earnestness in their domestic worship? This would at once be a concert in prayer. The history of those measures which led to our existing monthly Concert of Prayer (as it is called) is full of instruction and encouragement. In October, 1744, a number of Scottish ministers adopted a method for a limited period of two years, namely to set apart some time on Saturday evening, on the Lord's day morning, and more solemnly the first Tuesday of each quarter. Great numbers in Scotland and England fell in with the proposal, and some in America. In Edinburgh alone there were as many as thirty praying societies, some of which consisted of upwards of thirty members. The details are not here given because my intention is only to recommend the principle as applicable to domestic prayer. But there are some judicious remarks of Edwards, on the Scottish memorial respecting this subject, which are worthy of insertion as intimately connected with the very topic in hand.

"Union is one of the most amiable things that appertain to human society, yea, it is one of the most beautiful and happy things on earth which, indeed, makes earth most like heaven. God has made of one blood all nations of men, to dwell on all the face of the earth, hereby teaching us this moral lesson, that it becomes mankind all to be united as one family. And this is agreeable to the nature that God has given men, disposing them to society; and the circumstances God has placed them in, so many ways obliging and necessitating them to it. . . . As it is the glory of the Church of Christ that she, in all her members, however dispersed, is thus one holy society, one city, one family, one body, so it is very desirable that this union should be manifested and become visible, and so that here distant members should act as one in those things that concern the common interest of the whole body, and in those duties and exercises wherein they have to do with their common Lord and Head, as seeking of Him the common prosperity. It becomes all the members of a particular family who are so strictly united, and have in so many respects one common interest, to unite in prayer to God for the things they need; it becomes a nation, in days of prayer appointed by national authority, at certain seasons visibly to unite in prayer for those public mercies which concern the interest of the whole nation; so it becomes the Church of Christ, which is one holy nation, a peculiar people, one heavenly family, more strictly united in many respects, and having infinitely greater interests that are common to the whole than any other society visibly to unite, and expressly to agree together in prayer to God for the common prosperity."

There is nothing in such a proposal which may not be carried out in its principle by an agreement among Christian brethren in regard to their family worship. Thus, minding the same things, they would be drawn together by a tie of peculiar tenderness, and would feel all the binding influences of Christian friendship increased in strength.

In regard to the education of children who have already been dedicated to God in their baptism, no salutary influence can be considered small. Such children ought to grow up in the midst of prayers which may teach them how to pray. They should learn from the beginning to look, not on their own things only, but every one "also on the things of others," and to regard the Church of the Lord Jesus Christ as the great object of their affection, even from their earliest years. All the sentiments which, as I have said above, are cultivated by family worship are brought into the warm and ductile affections of the youthful heart among the most favorable circumstances. So that we are justified in expecting a marked difference, in respect to largeness of soul, expansive benevolence, and attachment to the church, between one who has passed his childhood in a house of prayer and one who has lived through that period of momentous interest among neglecters of God.

Can the Church willingly forego an instrument which promises these results? Can professors of faith in Christ deny themselves and their little ones a means of grace which God so blesses, or remain among the dangers of the "heathen, and the families that call not on His name?"

11

The Influence of Family Worship on the Commonwealth

To the earthly politician, nothing can seem more absurd than to ascribe to the devotions of private Christians any power in regard to states and empires. Religion is an element in political changes not recognized by the wisdom of this world. Yet it cannot be a matter of indifference, even in respect to civil government and national wealth, that hundreds of thousands of families, dispersed abroad in the earth, are daily addressing themselves to God in prayer. And it may turn out to be true that a nation in which all the families shall be thus employed will derive from this very peculiarity a character conducive to public strength.

Before treating the direct influence of prayer on nations, I wish to draw your attention to some particulars which are too much neglected. The indispensable material of a happy state is a body of good citizens. It is not territory, fertile soil, mines, cities, arts, navies, armies, monuments, laws, constitutions, or even liberty which sustain and ennoble a people, but good citizens. That which makes good citizens tends directly to the felicity and glory of a state. This will not be denied in an age and country of which it is the genius to flatter and almost deify the people. Viewing the matter even from the low point of temporal things, all admit that the power and stability of government reside in the virtue of the citizens.

This grand desideratum is to be secured not by wholesale enactment, but in detail. No general arrangements, however good, can reach the mind of the people. Legislation and polity presuppose good citizenship. National virtue is the virtue of collected individuals. The power to be applied for this result will therefore operate to most advantage when brought to bear on the primary and constituent portions, especially on each family and each individual.

To make good citizens we must begin early. It is too late when the adult character is attained—hence the acknowledged importance of universal education in a free country. But this early training may be complete in respect of intellectual discipline, and may yet be inadequate. We need moral qualities in good citizens. If we could so descend to the elements of society as to make every family a school of sound principles and virtuous habits, we would plainly be dealing with the very factors and constituents of a prosperous state; and the method which would accomplish this would be a national blessing. Such a method is domestic religion, including as one of its principal parts family worship. We are prepared to maintain that this institution cannot flourish in any country without directly contributing to those habits which are favorable to law, order, and peace.

It is no more true that the infant brood grows to the power of caring for themselves in the nest than that men are formed into the habits of life in the family. It is the earliest, cheapest, safest, and mightiest institution for this purpose. Hence it is the special object of assault from the gathering hordes of disorganizing reformers in our day. On every side we hear the outcry against the domestic temple: "Raze it, raze it, even to the foundations thereof" (Psalm 137:7). Ignorant of the true sources of pauperism and oppression, our ruling pseudo-philanthropists are in perpetual agitation about the wrongs of labor, the rights of women, and the reconstruction of society. "Association," such as they propose, would pluck away the hearth stone, and break the marriage ring. Forgetful of the homely sentence that the largest house is not large enough for two families, they would take down all partitions, throw a whole community into one, cashier the natural guardians of infancy, and subject masses of youth, in phalanxes, to the regimental drill of a newly-invented education. As bubble after bubble explodes, and successive prophets of Socialism fall into deserved contempt, it is hoped that the world will become satisfied with the constitution which dates back as far as Paradise.

Every Christian household is a school of good citizenship. This might be safely rested on reasons already given. But one or two particulars merit separate consideration. Family worship, as we have seen, promotes habits of order. It brings a stated regulation into the house and gathers the inmates by a fixed law. It sets up a wholesome barrier against wanton irregularity, sloth, and night-wandering. It encourages early hours, thoughtfulness, and affection; and above all it adds strength to the principle of subordination and obedience, a point which we dare not pass lightly.

Good citizens are such as abide by the law and submit themselves to authority. The habit of so doing must be formed under the parental roof. All the duties of subjects and citizens range themselves under the fifth commandment; and he who is not a good son cannot be a good citizen. Here we may refer to a passage already cited, in which God says of Abraham, "I know him, that he will command his children and his household after him" (Genesis 18:19). Domestic discipline is an ordinance of God. As the family was the earliest community, so this is the earliest form of government; and, notwithstanding the dreams of Rousseau and his disciples about a social contract which never existed, here is the true origin of states. Observe the connection: "Abram shall surely become a great and mighty nation; for I know him, that he will command his children." Here is the influence of family religion on the commonwealth. We have already said enough to show the bearing of domestic worship on parental control and filial obedience; our present inquiry is in regard to the tendency of this to public safety and peace.

The popular evils which threaten our country arise in great measure from a spirit of insubordination; and this is caused by neglect of parental authority. He who has never learned to obey and honor his father and his mother will never yield himself to magistracy and law. The evil is bold and increasing. Children become men with a frightful precocity. Travelers from abroad complain that there are no boys among us, only infants and men; the period of subordination is overleaped. In our cities the streets are filled with hordes of urchins who appear to acknowledge no loyalty to any household. These are the materials for mobs and insurrections, the candidates for jails and gibbets, almshouses, and vessels of piracy. It is needless to say that the houses from which such youth proceed enjoy no worship of God; but I conceive it to be important to add that the conscientious observance of family devotions will go far to prevent such enormities. A nation of families worshipping God will ever be a nation of law and order.

No municipal police can make up for the absence of domestic authority. The weakening of this principle over a whole land is nothing but the rupture of each several link in the chain. As the evil advances, we lose the very material of magistracy and the capacity for firm and gentle command.

The scriptural maxim is that he who cannot rule at home cannot rule abroad. The bishop or minister must be "one that ruleth well his own house, having his children in subjection with all gravity; for if a man know not how to rule his own house, how shall he take care of the Church of God?" (1 Timothy 3:5). The principle admits of an equal application to civil government. The discipline of the family cannot be invaded without a corresponding disorganization of society. And the great end is to be attained not by adding strength to government, stringency to laws, or terror to punishments, but by training in every house in the land a group of Christian citizens habituated to manly obedience.

We have still to consider the great and crowning favor which family worship confers on the commonwealth: it brings down heavenly blessings from the prayer-hearing God.

Take out of a nation its praying souls, and you leave it defenseless and accursed. Cities and kingdoms have been spared for the sake of Christ's people who were in them. Jehovah would have withheld His destroying vengeance from Sodom and the cities of the plain "for ten's sake" (Genesis 18:32). The cries of the poor who fear God "enter into the ears of the Lord of Sabaoth" (James 5:4). Politicians attribute no potency to the prayers of believers, but they are heard in heaven. They have, before now, averted great evils and procured great deliverances. Israel was about to be utterly consumed at Taberah, but "when Moses prayed unto the Lord, the fire was quenched" (Numbers 11:2). The agonizing prayer of Daniel for his people was mighty before God (Daniel 10:14). When the Most High is about to return to a guilty people, He does it in answer to prayer, and summons those who fear Him to humiliation. "Let the bridegroom go forth of his chamber, and the bride out of her closet; let the priests, the Lord's ministers, weep between the porch and the altar, and let them say, 'Spare Thy people, O Lord' " (Joel 2:16–17). The angel who stands with a drawn sword over a country is no doubt often recalled by reason of those prayers which are forgotten by sinful rulers and a profane people.

True Christians feel it to be their bounden duty to pray for the government. Though we have no prescribed liturgical form for this in our public service, we hold it to be an important part of intercession. We have known ministers to be charged with partisanship in politics because they publicly prayed for the chief magistrate. No patriot and no Christian can consistently refuse so to pray with fullness and earnestness. It would be dreadful, indeed, if the devotions of God's house were to take their direction from the gusts of political opinion. It is no human rubric, but an inspired oracle which enjoins that "supplications, prayers, intercessions, and giving of thanks be made for all men; for kings, and for all that are in authority; that we may lead a peaceable life, in all godliness and honesty" (1 Timothy 2:1–2). Such prayers go up from the devout household also, and, the more they are multiplied, the more reason is there to hope for national prosperity.

Men who love their country will delight to take their households with them to the throne of grace, in beseeching God's favor in any great national emergency. When questions of vast moment are in suspense, when divisions are threatened, especially when the country is at war, the prayers of Christian families in every church throughout the land are exerting an unseen agency, outweighing, perhaps, the deliberations of senates, cabinets, and councils of war. And the youth who are trained to such prayers are growing up in the best school of patriotism. No man will be less likely to love his country for having been taught to pray for it every day.

A land covered by praying families may be well called "a Christian land." That it would be happy in proportion, even in civil affairs, can be denied only by those who reject all religion. Were every town in America, in this respect, what Kidderminster was in the days of Baxter, we should, indeed, be the glory of all lands. It is all that we need for our exaltation, and the method by which it is to be sought is not remote or recondite, not the method of association or agitation, or waiting for others to concur; it is simply for every man in his place to set up the worship of God. The true way to bring health to a diseased nation is to carry the cure to every house. The aggregate energy of a multitude of zealous families, untied in prayer for the country, is beyond all computation; it is this which "exalteth a nation." Patriotism could confer nothing better on the land she loves than to kindle this fire on every hearth. The voice of thanksgiving and joy would burst over the domestic and national walls, and reach the most distant lands. Who will not pray for such a consummation? "Let the people praise Thee, O God; let all the people praise Thee. Then shall the earth yield her increase; and God, even our own God, shall bless us. God shall bless us; and all the ends of the earth shall fear Him" (Psalm 67:5–7).

12

The Influence of Family Worship on Posterity

He was a bumpkin who said, "Why should I care for posterity? What has posterity done for me?" Only a mean and selfish mind can be indifferent to what is coming on the earth. If any such meaning was involved in the obscure words of King Hezekiah, he was certainly not generous in his thoughts when, on hearing the sentence of God, he exclaimed, "Is it not good, if peace and truth be in my days?" (2 Kings 20:19). We take pleasure in receiving the words in a nobler sense. There are men, however, whose maxim is, "Let us eat and drink, for tomorrow we die" (1 Corinthians 15:32). They close their eyes to everything which may happen after they are gone, content to live in self-indulgence, and to let their children take their chance.

The religion of the Bible sets itself in stern opposition to such a temper. It constantly directs our view to children, and children's children, teaching us that all the good which we have is to be transmitted. The Church, the Bible, and the Sacraments are made a part of this chain. Our children are brought to baptism, as the sons of ancient believers were brought to circumcision, that they may be introduced into this series; and the blessings of the Church are a sacred trust for remote ages. True patriotism speaks the same language. The fathers of our constitution provided for contingencies yet in reserve and far distant; and wise legislation is perpetually endeavoring to pierce the future and secure the welfare of the country when the present generation shall be no more. Institutions which hold out a promise of good to those who shall come after us cannot but be dear to the patriot and the parent. Natural affection and parental piety are far-sighted, and look down the misty prospect with an anxious gaze. No man who is worthy of the name of a father can be unconcerned in regard to the destiny of his children, or even his remote descendants. This consideration has entered largely into the legal usages and statutes of all nations, and especially colors the common law of our ancestors. We observe it in the primogeniture and entails of England, and in all that relates to the tenure of lands. It is remarkably operative in all testamentary disposition of estates. Those who accumulate property are chiefly influenced by a regard for their offspring, and, when they can no longer enjoy it themselves, leave no cautions unobserved in order to secure it to their families. Rising to a level of higher benevolence, we observe the principle operating in charitable bequests and endowments, and in the founding of institutions which are known to be capable of only a partial influence in the present day. It is the chief function of governments to provide for this very result, to be realized long after those who make and administer the laws have passed from human things.

It cannot have escaped the observation of any reflective mind that, among the links which connect the existing race with posterity, the most essential is the family. It is, indeed, the very point of connection. The whole series is resolvable into the natural sequence of father and son. For which reason divine Providence has seized upon this relation as the channel for conveying down the blessings of religion, as we may observe in numerous rites and institutions. I regard family worship as one of the most important of these.

While it is true that all religious institutions affect posterity, it is more eminently true that those institutions have this tendency which bear primarily and directly on the family connection. If the piety of any man is likely to carry its impulse into coming years, more signally will that piety do so which, through sovereign grace, flows from the father to the child, and above all in those particular acts which concern the education of the child. We never aim so immediately at the next generation as when we govern the parental influence; it is directing and purifying the spring before it widens into the stream. The geometrical ratio of human increase adds force to this consideration, and shows that in the economy of means we work at a great advantage when we secure any good to the prolific source of multitudes of men. It is, therefore, far more hopeful to pour truth and holiness on a single household now than to found a system which shall address its influence to hundreds half a century hence. Family religion gathers fresh importance when we extend our views a little into the future.

It has pleased God to have special regard to the transmission of religion by domestic means. His covenant is from father to son. He is the God of Abraham, of Isaac, and of Jacob. Circumcision was the "token of the covenant" between Jehovah and His people (Genesis 17:11). The Pass-over was a family rite. It had regard to posterity. "Ye shall observe this thing for an ordinance to thee and to thy sons forever" (Exodus 12:24). It was a part of the annual family worship of Israel. It was a means of instruction for the perpetuation of the truth. "It shall come to pass, when your children shall say unto you, 'What mean ye by this service?' that ye shall say, 'It is the sacrifice of the Lord's Passover, who passed over the houses of the children of Israel in Egypt, when He smote the Egyptians and delivered our houses' " (Exodus 12:26–27). Infant baptism, which has come in the place of the ancient initiation under the enlarged privileges of the Christian church, has not abandoned the principle, but involves the obligation of parents to pray with and for their children, and to bring them up in the nurture and admonition of the Lord.

The gracious promises of God to His Church, while they do not necessarily transmit salvation in the line of natural descent, perpetually recognize the relation of parent and child. God determines that His great favors shall descend from age to age. "The promise is to you and to your children." From the beginning of the world, He has dealt with mankind on the family principal. Every covenant has comprised succeeding generations. The federal and representative element, variously modified, is in every system from Eden to Pentecost. It is breathed in the first promise; it beams in the bow of Ararat; it fills the starry page of Abraham (Genesis 15:5); it is uttered through the fires of Sinai; it is inscribed on the bloody lintel of Egypt; it flows in the household baptism of the New Testament. God, in His sovereign pleasure, makes the parental and filial relation the means of great blessing in natural things. He is further pleased to sanctify it and use it as a vehicle for heavenly things. He might have saved us singly, in insulation, plucking one and another from the corrupt, perishing mass. It would have been infinite grace! But, blessed be His name, He has decreed otherwise. The "word of this life" is not a cistern, but a fountain; and it flows from father to child. Not that by natural descent or inheritance we can convey this deposit. Not that the succession is always unbroken. Even here Jehovah reserves a place for the display of His sovereignty, and a motive for the diligence of the parent. Ah, we cannot forget the names of Hophni and Phinehas, of Amnon and Absalom! Yet the principle abides. Branches may die, but the tree still flourishes. Families may die out, but the race is not extinct. Nay, more, it is remarkable how generally and how widely religion descends in the line of father and son. There is everything to encourage prayer and faithful training, and living hope, even while we are not allowed to look for the salvation of our children as a matter of course.

Here is our chief hope for posterity. This kindles an altar of perpetual fire in the house. This lightens our faces when we hold our little ones for the affusion of baptism. This revives our souls when we fold their hands in ours as they kneel beside us. This consecrates the delightful moment when their lisping words first echo to us the name of "Jesus." This spreads a canopy of promise over the morning and the evening group in the tabernacle of prayer. And this lifts us above ourselves when we catch a Sabbath glimpse of the towers of the sanctuary, and lead our chief treasures along the way; when the little hand throbs in ours, and we say, "Come, let us go up to the house of the Lord."

It is by the salvation of the children of the Church more than from all other means that we hope for the salvation of the world. It is by this very method, as we observe in history, that the word of grace has been carried abroad from land to land and brought down to us. Amidst many seeming failures, the holy seed is kept up. Take the darkest view: there is scarcely a Christian family in a thousand of those who daily worship God in which one member does not maintain the succession, while there are thousands of which every member is a visible believer. The stream often runs under ground. The descendants of the first converts are possibly on earth now. Within a very few years the descendants of Luther, whose life was thought extinct, have been picked up in Germany, poor and squalid, to be embraced by

Christian charity. There are clergymen now in the Scottish church who have descended from an unbroken line not only of believers, but of ministers: and there is a blessed instance in our own communion of six living preachers of the gospel, all "sons of one man," himself a servant of the sanctuary. He who preserves the seed of Abraham, though sifted among all nations, will find it easy to preserve his spiritual seed. When the terms of this covenant are, by divine power, made to take effect by means of Christian education, holy example, and family prayer, the increase is often manifold in that astonishing, redoubling proportion which is a law of human growth. Thus the tree spreads its boughs and scatters its fruit; the original blessing does not die in the hands of those who receive it, but is widely communicated. And the latter glory shall be a period when, as we think, the promise shall be accomplished universally. "As the days of a tree are the days of My people, and they shall long enjoy the work of their hands. They shall not labor in vain, nor bring forth for trouble, for they are the seed of the blessed of the Lord, and their children with them" (Isaiah 65:22).

A few years ago there met upon the platform of one of our great benevolent societies, on an anniversary, a grandson of Isabella Graham and a grandson of John Brown of Haddington, both warm in aid of the blessed cause, and both eminent ministers of the gospel, though in different hemispheres. A Christian lady whose "works praise her in the gates," and whom this author is thankful to number among his flock, sent up to the treasurer a billet enclosing her contribution, marked with these words: " 'As for Me, this is my covenant with them,' saith the Lord. 'My Spirit that is upon thee, and My words which I have put in thy mouth, shall not depart out of thy mouth, nor out of the mouth of thy seed, nor out of the mouth of thy seed's seed,' saith the Lord, 'from henceforth and forever' " (Isaiah 59:21).

In our visions of good for our beloved land, we look upon vast tracts of yet uninhabited country, stretching over the mountains to the Pacific Ocean, as to be peopled by a mighty nation, such as the world has never seen comprehended in one polity. The tribute of many kingdoms is pouring its tide of population. But shall it be Christian or unchristian? This is the forming period; and these new societies are taking their mold and direction. Public means of instruction can by no effort keep pace with the colossal strides of population. Yet among those who migrate to these unbroken wastes, there are some who have been bred in the school of domestic piety in Europe or America. What can they do better for their children, or better for their country, than to found the "church in the house?" In the absence of other means, they will thus be leaving the best inheritance to their children—one that is infinitely better than gold or silver. Five years ago, this writer procured, at the clerk's office of Charlotte county in Virginia, a certified extract from the last will of the great orator and patriot, Patrick Henry. It is in these words: "This is all the inheritance I can give to my dear family; the religion of Christ can give them one which will make them rich indeed." This is the provision which we recommend to our brethren in new countries to make for posterity. Colonies and settlements founded in prayer will have a blessing. Those who emigrate are sometimes more concerned about the richness of the soil and the salubrity of the climate than about the spiritual advancement of their house. Their error is like that of Lot (Genesis 13:10). The young race grows up without a sanctuary. How invaluable in such situations is domestic worship! It may go far to supply the public ministration of the Word; it will certainly draw down family blessings from the Hearer of prayer; it will make itself felt in coming generations. The God of Abraham, Isaac, and Jacob answers the prayers of departed saints who still "live unto Him" (Luke 20:38). Posterity reaps harvests from seed sown in the tears of former ages. We are, perhaps, this day receiving blessings in answer to the prayers of our forefathers, offered in the glens and moors of the old world. There is encouragement to extend as widely as possible the daily supplications of Christian families.

No pious heart can fail to be transported at the prospect of a whole nation of praying houses. It is possible with God. It is a consummation worth striving for, and worth a more distinct, energetic, and unified effort than the church has yet put forth. Every approximation towards it should be hailed with delight. Every church court, every pastor, missionary, and ruling elder, every Sabbath-school teacher, and colporteur, out of love for the generation to come, should make the establishment of family worship an object of separate and earnest endeavor. Every father of a family should consider himself as charged with the souls of those whom he hopes to leave behind him, and as contributing to the future propagation of the truth by every act of devotion performed in his house. Wherever he has a tent, God should have an altar. Every professing Christian who has hitherto lived in neglect of this great duty of a household should repent, humble himself, and establish God's service at his fireside before he sleeps another night in a prayerless dwelling. Such resolutions, efforts, and devotions will do more for the happiness of that exceeding great multitude of future Americans, whom some compute at a hundred million souls, than all the accumulations of family wealth, all the internal improvements, all the legislation of States and of the Union, and all the schemes of general education. We cannot close our eyes to the dangers which threaten our country from an augmentation of the people without a corresponding growth of piety. The church must lose its vital warmth and power unless some new impulse be given from within, and among the means for kindling this central fire, I reckon family worship to be not the least. In the conflict of our hopes and fears, we think we may see a ray of brightness in the expectation that Christ's people will awaken to consider the power of an instrument which is within their very doors; which operates directly on the objects of their most tender love; which will be carried down the stream of time by their increasing progeny; which will bless the race which is unborn; and which will still subsist in its triumphant vigor when the Lord shall come. The treasure in our hands has been conveyed to us from those who were our fathers according to the flesh. It was coeval with the Reformation; it was held dear by our suffering ancestors in the British Isles; it was delivered over by confessors and martyrs to their children; it is in its very nature fit for transmission; it must not perish in our charge. No! With the help of the Lord, we will convey His testimonies, and the record of His mighty deeds, to our offspring. "We will not hide them from their children, showing to the generation to come the praises of the Lord, and His strength, and His wonderful works that He hath done; that the generation to come might know them, even the children which should be born, who should arise and declare them to their children, that they might set their hope in God, and not forget the works of God, but keep His commandments" (Psalm 78:4, 6–7).

A new dignity shines around the simple daily worship of the lowliest Christian cottage, when we regard it as one

of the most direct means for perpetuating the love and service of God through our descendants to the whole land,
and the universal race of man. Afflicted and tempest-tossed
Zion has this word of reviving promise: "All thy children
shall be taught of the Lord, and great shall be the peace of
thy children" (Isaiah 54:13).

13

*Practical Directions as to the Mode
of Conducting Family Worship*

To one who is conscientiously resolved to honor God in his household, a clear conception of the duty itself, and some method in the observance of it, are indispensable.

The very first question which offers itself is, "By whom is this service to be rendered?" To this the name itself is a reply: it is *family* worship. All the dwellers in one house. More particularly, the parents, the children (or such as occupy the children's place, such as wards, pupils, or apprentices), the lodgers, and other inmates: the guests and sojourners, and the servants.

The duty of masters has been already explained. Let it suffice here to say that every Christian householder should acknowledge his solemn obligation to extend the blessings of domestic religion to his servants as much as to his children. All proper means should be used to secure the attendance of every individual engaged in the labor of the family, even if this should render it needful to sacrifice some momentary convenience in regard to meals and other arrangements. The beauty of this service depends in no small degree on the presence of the whole family. The reverse of this is too common, and there are houses where, from sloth or irreligion, some members habitually absent themselves from the prayers. Even in boarding-houses and inns, I have known the most happy effects to flow from the practice of gathering all who were under the roof at the time of worship. It is also a good usage to proceed with the accustomed devotion, even though casual visitors may be present. Providence may thus be opening a door for unexpected influence.

The time for family worship demands our consideration. By common consent, the Christian world has allotted to it the two seasons of morning and evening; not that there is any virtue in this number or in these seasons, but because it seems just and fit to place our acknowledgment of God at these natural terms of our working day. There have been those who have found edification in three hours of prayer: "Evening and morning, and at noon, will I pray, and cry aloud, and He shall hear my voice" (Psalm 55:17).

That which is most important in regard to the time of family worship is that it should be fixed. We ascribe great value to this particular. It adds dignity to the service by showing that it is not to give way to the changes or caprice of business or amusement. It saves the time of the household; and it tends to that method and punctuality in domestic affairs which is a chief ornament of a Christian home.

Morning prayer should be, in my humble judgment, early in the morning. Here there is diversity of usage, and I am not of those who would impose my own preferences on others, or invent any ceremonial yoke. But I have noted striking advantages in observing family devotion at as early an hour as the whole household can be assembled. There is a Christian decorum in resorting to God before we gather around the table of His bounty. The refreshment of food seems to acquire a blessing, "for it is sanctified by the Word of God and prayer" (1 Timothy 4:5). It appears right to seek food for the soul before we seek food for the body.

Otherwise we lose the delightful feeling of having begun the day with God. The moment of repletion from a meal is, of all others, the least comely for a solemn approach to heaven. Moreover, by seizing an early hour, we avoid numerous interruptions and that sense of hurry and impatience which attend the time immediately preceding the forenoon's business. All these reasons may, however, be controlled by considerations of health and business, and every man must be left to his own judgment.

Evening prayer is, of course, the closing domestic service. Hence it has been the prevalent custom to make it the last thing before retiring for the night; and there is certainly something beautiful in the arrangement. In many houses it is the only time which can be secured. Yet it must be acknowledged that there is a practical difficulty connected with this; and family worship may be too late for those who, agreeably to our view of the subject, are principally concerned, to wit, servants and, especially, children. The younger members of a family are apt to be unfit for the service, as being overcome with sleep; and it is scarcely just that they should be robbed of one half of domestic prayer, as they must be if they retire at an early hour. Even adults are often disqualified for enjoying the work of praise by the weariness and stupor consequent on a long day of toil. Hence some have thought they found an advantage in calling together the family immediately before or immediately after the evening meal. It is a laudable method; but here, as in all things connected with form, we would ask and give the largest liberty, only "let all things be done decently, and in order" (1 Corinthians 14:40).

The person whose office it is to lead in family worship is undoubtedly the head of the household. The father is here in his proper place as the prophet and patriarch of his little state. In the occasional absence of the father, or in the lamented event of his removal, Providence has devolved this, with all other parental trusts, on the solitary or widowed mother. And though it brings with it a keen trial to diffidence and feminine reserve, it is also eminently amiable and touching; and dutiful sons will make every sacrifice in order to lessen the burdens of the maternal heart when engaged in such a duty. The parent may sometimes see cause to dispute this office to a son or brother when the latter, from education, gifts, or graces, is qualified to take his part with edification. In a house which is so happy as to comprise several such persons, rotation in the service may be allowed—always reserving to the father, or head, his prerogative and responsibility of direction.

The constituent parts of family worship, when fully observed, are, first, the reading of the Scriptures; second, singing praise to God; and, third, prayer. And these may very properly follow each other in this order. But I propose to enlarge on these particulars below.

The length of the domestic service is worthy of attention. It was the fault of our forefathers to make it insufferably long. This goes far to destroy all good influence on the young by creating weariness and disgust. "It is difficult," says Cecil, "to fix and quiet your family. The servants are eager to be gone, to do something in hand. There has been some disagreement, perhaps, between them and their mistress. We must seize opportunities. We must not drive hard at such times as these. Religion should be prudently brought before a family. The old Dissenters wearied their families. Jacob reasoned well with Esau about the tenderness of his children, and his flocks and herds. Something gentle, quiet, and moderate should be our aim" (Cecil's *Remains*).

The manner and spirit of the service should never be neglected. In every part it should be solemn, and fitted to repress all levity. Of course, every secular task or amusement will be suspended, and absolute silence and quiet will be enforced, even in the case of the youngest children, who thereby gain a most important lesson. The greatest simplicity should characterize every word and every petition. Those who have the greatest interest in the worship are often little more than babes. But we would especially recommend a holy animation as that which will arrest attention and make way for pleasant memories. Here again I avail myself of the language of Rev. Richard Cecil. Speaking of children and servants he says, "Tediousness will weary them. Fine language will shoot above them. Formality of connection or composition in prayer, they will not comprehend. Gloominess, or austerity of devotion, will make them think it a hard service. Let them be met with smiles. Let them be met as friends. Let them be met as for the most delightful service in which they can be engaged. Let them find it short, savory, simple, plain, tender, and heavenly. I find it easy to keep the attention of a congregation compared with that of my family."

Prayer is the essential part of family worship, and therefore merits the first place in our consideration. It is not necessary to enlarge on those things which are common to all acts of prayer; these belong to another subject. That which concerns us is family prayer. This, its distinguishing character, ought never to be out of sight. It is the worship of those who are joined together by Providence as dwellers in the same house, and who now come to the throne of grace in their family capacity. This will give a tinge to the whole service, where it is conducted with life and discrimination. Many things may be proper here which would be out of place in a promiscuous assembly, or even a small meeting. There is no domestic want, danger, sorrow, or dispensation which may not be remembered. Special cases in the household will be faithfully and affectionately commended to God, but without that rudeness and irreverence with which we have known vulgar minds to drag forward the circumstances, and even names of shrinking individuals. But our Heavenly Father permits us to spread before Him our minutest trials, and this is one of the principal blessings of domestic religion.

What has been said of brevity applies especially to prayer as a part of family worship. Few things are more hardening and deadening in their influence than the daily recurrence of long and unawakening prayers. For these there is no necessity. For while family prayer includes petitions for blessings far more wide than those of the family alone, it may be comprised within easy limits; and nothing will so much tend to this as earnestness and directness in supplication. The prayer should be, by all means, simple and intelligible; free from hard words and involved periods; because he who leads is putting words into the mouths of children. The best model is found in the brief and childlike petitions which we find in the Psalms, and other parts of Scripture.

Family prayer should be varied; otherwise the inevitable result will be formalism and tediousness. Indeed the snare into which we are most prone to fall in this service is that of sameness and routine. Daily changes in the condition of a family will infallibly work a corresponding change in the prayers, if they are sincere. Nothing will really secure this needful quality but the "spirit of grace and of supplications" shed down from on high, which should, therefore, be most earnestly sought by every head of a household, with reference to this daily service. For this purpose, no preparation can be so valuable as attendance on the previous devotions of the closet.

The question has been much agitated whether any forms of prayer should be recommended as a help to family devotions. The spirit of our church institutions, and our perpetual testimony, has been against the imposition of any prescribed form, and in favor of entire liberty in prayer. I am fully persuaded that the best of all prayers in the family, as everywhere else, are those which precede, without book, from hearts which God has touched. And my unhesitating counsel to everyone who essays this duty is that he cast himself upon the help of the Spirit, without any written form. Nevertheless, I am so earnestly desirous to remove every hindrance out of the way even of halting believers that I would infinitely rather they should pray with a form than that they should not pray at all. There are also persons of such diffidence, especially of the female sex, or in so peculiar a condition of society, that they feel themselves utterly unable to proceed without such assistance. Let such go forward in the name of the Lord. [*The Book of Common Order*, often called "John Knox's Liturgy," contains a "Form of Prayers, to be used in private houses every morning and evening."] Let them provide themselves with some suitable volume of family rayers. Such have been furnished by Messrs. Jenks, Thornton, Hardman, and others. The work of Mr. Jenks is by far superior to anything known to me of this sort, being warm, orthodox, and scriptural, and imbued from beginning to end with evangelical sentiments [*Prayers and Offices of Devotion for Families, and for particular persons, upon most occasions,* by Benjamin Jenks, late Rector of Harley. Altered and improved by the Rev. Charles Simeon, late Fellow of King's College, Cambridge. About forty editions of this work have been published; and Mr. Simeon well says, "Its distinguishing excellency is that far the greater part of the prayers appear to have been prayed and not written."] But, in the use of this or any other form, the greatest caution is necessary in order to guard against that ritual coldness and emptiness which come from the abuse of the best devotional compositions.

If I had not known cases where such a counsel was needful, I would scarcely add that the true posture for family prayer is that of kneeling.

It only remains to be observed that if the father of a family would make this service one of the greatest advantage, he must deem it worthy of being in his thoughts at moments when he is not actually engaged in it. He will seek to keep his mind in such a frame as not to make him unfit to lead his children to God. He will look to his steps lest his example should be in disastrous contrast with his devotional acts. And he will not consider it unimportant to seek from God special direction and strength for the discharge of a duty so nearly connected with the everlasting interests of his house.

Where any one feels himself called of God to establish daily worship in his house, he should act with solemn decision. In this, as in a thousand other affairs of life, the shortest method is the best. Instead of parleying with objections, or waiting for some happy conjuncture, or seeking to prepare the way by gradual approaches, or timorously sounding the opinions of those whose place it is to submit, let him, in reliance on God, without other preliminaries, and without allowing another sun to set, call his family together, state his purpose in the very fewest terms, and carry it into immediate accomplishment. The burden of months or years will have rolled away! That day will be remembered as one of the brightest in his calendar, and will probably open a new era of domestic profit and joy. If this book should fall into the hands of young persons and others, who live in families where God is daily worshipped, let them be affectionately exhorted to yield all possible encouragement to the service by punctual attendance, by the most reverent attention and devout silence, and, above all, by heartily joining in the devotions, so that the words spoken or sung may convey the sentiments of their own hearts. This is especially to be urged on the children of the church, who ought to remember that in this service their honored parents are endeavoring, often with a deep sense of unworthiness, to discharge a part of the obligations which were recognized at the baptism of their children. Many, however, are the instances in which a father, advanced in years, needing repose, and trembling in voice and every limb, is left to wait till a late hour of night for forward and profane sons who, if the truth were known, would gladly come in at midnight rather than be constrained to join in prayer. Let it be added, in conclusion, that filial affection will certainly lead the ingenuous son or daughter to repress every feeling to the manner in which a parent conducts the worship of the house.

14

The Reading of Scripture as a Part of Family Worship

The reading of the Word of God in the daily service of the house seems entitled to a brief, separate consideration. But after having already given such extent to our discussion, allow me to omit many of those remarks, however important, and which should be sought in other books. The daily reading of Scripture is a solemn and indispensable part of family worship, one which I cannot consent to see omitted in any case. To do so under pretext of saving time, or for any other reason, except in extreme occasions, is a wrong done to the household. The greatest misapprehensions prevail in regard to the extent of knowledge thus communicated. If a man had no other information of God's will than that which was conveyed by hearing a portion read twice a day, all his life, he might nevertheless acquire not merely the sum of saving truth for his own soul's welfare, but a body of invaluable Christian instruction. But when we consider it as so much added to all other means of knowledge, we ought to admit that the agency is one too potent to be neglected. In every family there are those who daily hear who yet have no ability or no willingness to read. To some, this is the only means of acquaintance with God's Word. To all, it brings that Word before the mind under the most favorable circumstances. Truth is thus gently pressed upon the heart of infancy and youth at a time when that heart is most ductile, and when it takes its most lasting mold. If we ask ourselves what are our earliest recollections in regard to the Scriptures, some of us will have to answer that they are of incidents or expressions heard at family worship. Much more than is commonly thought is actually understood by children, though not, perhaps, in that precise order which might be prescribed by pragmatical reforms in education. There is an absurd rage in some for making juvenile training a school of perpetual lexicography. Children may comprehend many a paragraph without being able to "define" every word. There is such a thing as outline knowledge, which precedes the filling up of details: it is the method of nature; it is the way in which constant hearing of the word informs the infant mind. Even the high points of the range of Christian truth may cast their shadows over the child. A little one may gain life-long impressions from a great physical object, as from Niagara, or the Natural Bridge, though utterly incompetent to describe it; but no less truly may he derive truth from a great event, or a great argument of Scripture, though unprepared to stand an examination on it. Besides, there are a thousand things in the Bible which are just as level to the babe as to the philosopher.

No trifling advantage is gained when the mind is, from infancy, made familiar with the phraseology of Scripture. Persons who have been religiously educated often do not know how much there is in these venerated expressions which carry no meaning, or convey strange associations, to such as have not learned them in youth. Such an evil is effectually prevented by family reading of the Word. The acquaintance of Scottish peasants with the text of inspiration is proverbial, and it is a noble foundation for that structure which is to be carried up by subsequent labors. The Word

of God is quite a different book to him who can recall no
day in which he did not hear it read; as each of us may as-
sure himself by reflecting on the emotions raised within
him by that single term, "the family Bible."

When asked how much of the Scripture is to be read in
family worship, I reply, "the whole Bible." Not that any
Judaic superstition should be allowed to creep in, as though
we were bound to refuse all selection, or to persevere
through whole chapters of proper names and genealogies.
Still, in general terms, I would say, the whole Bible. And I
leaning to the side of those who make no omissions, rather
than to the fastidiousness which would exclude large portions of the sacred Record.

The order in which Scripture should be read in family
worship may safely be left to that wisdom which "is profitable to direct." It is a wholesome rule which prescribes the
New Testament for the morning and the Old Testament
for the evening, and which goes through these in regular
order, with such variations as circumstances and providen-
tial tokens may indicate. At least one chapter may be read
at one time, carefully observing that the existing division of
chapters is a human arrangement, and that it often breaks
the current of discourse. I am not ignorant of the numerous
plans, such as that of the late Mr. McCheyne, for complet-
ing the whole Bible in a single twelve months. But after
trial and reflection, I am disposed to regard them all as at-
tributing an undue importance to the compassing of this
work in the exact term of a calendar year; and I choose
rather to leave this, with many similar details, to the discre-
tion of the "wise householder" (Luke 12:42).

The judgment of such a man as Philip Henry, in regard
to the order of reading, is worthy of record. "He advised the
reading of the Scripture in order; for though one star in the

firmament of the Scripture differs from another star in glory, yet wherever God has a mouth to speak we should have an ear to hear; and the diligent searcher may find much excellent matter in those parts of Scripture which we are sometimes tempted to think might have been spared. How affectionately would he sometimes bless God for every book, chapter, verse, and line in the Bible" (*Life of Philip Henry*, p. 87, edition of the Presbyterian Board of Publication). To this I may add the testimony of Mr. Cecil: "I read the Scriptures to my family in some regular order, and am pleased to have thus a lesson found for me. I look on the chapter of the day as a lesson sent for that day; and so I regard it as coming from God for the use of that day, and not of my own seeking" (Cecil's *Works*, iii:337).

How far the portion of Scripture which is read shall be expounded must depend on the gifts of the officiating person, and the circumstances and character of his family. The all-important thing undoubtedly is the Word of revelation. Yet it is good to have everything which may render this more plain or carry it to the heart. Situated as most families are, the continuous reading of an entire commentary is scarcely to be thought of. Great profit has, however, been derived from skillful selections from such works as Scott's *Notes*, Matthew Henry's *Commentaries*, the humbler works of Burkitt, Ostervald, and Brown, Doddridge's *Expositor*, and Horne on the Psalms. The author of *Line upon Line* has produced a convenient manual of select passages with comments for this very purpose, entitled, *Light in the Dwelling*. Other books, not commentaries, may be occasionally used in short portions, such as William Jay's *Morning and Evening Exercises*, John Mason's *Spiritual Treasury*, and Robert Hawker's *Poor Man's Morning Portion*. On the Lord's Day, where there is no public worship, it is exceedingly to be desired that Christian families should add to their usual service the reading of a good sermon; it would, above all things else, make up for the lack of more stated ordinances.

Oral exposition by the father of the family is a more difficult work, and should not be attempted without due consideration. It is certainly desirable that a passing remark should now and then be thrown in to explain a hard word, prevent a misconception, or apply a divine sentence to the heart. "I make no formal comment on the Scripture," says Mr. Cecil, "but when any striking event or sentiment arises, I say, 'Mark that! See how God judges of that thing!' Sometimes I ask what they think of the matter, and how such a thing strikes them." A suitable pause after some remarkable passage is often itself a comment. The father may often with profit select a verse or more from the morning lesson to be meditated on or committed to memory during the day (from the notes taken on domestic exposition, the pious daughters of a living minister have found materials for a published volume. I allude to *Family Expositions on the Epistles of St. John and St. Jude* by Rev. E. Bickersteth, rector of Wotton, Herts. London, 1846).

There are certain persons who, by their station or their gifts, may seem called upon to enter more freely than others upon the work of exposition. Here we would again cite Philip Henry: "What he read in his family he always expounded, and exhorted all ministers to do so, as an excellent means of increasing their acquaintance with the Scriptures. His expositions were not so much critical as plain, practical, useful, and such as tended to edification, and to answer the end for which the Scriptures were written, which is to make us wise unto salvation. And herein he had a peculiar excellence, performing that daily exercise with so much judgment, and at the same time with such facility and clearness, as if every exposition had been premeditated; and very instructive they were, as well as affecting to the auditors. He often admired that saying of Tertullian's, 'I adore the fullness of the Scriptures.' When sometimes he had hit upon some useful observation that was new to him, he would say afterwards to those about him, 'How often have I read this chapter, and never before now took notice of such a thing in it!' He put his children, while they were with him, to write these expositions; and when they were gone from him, the strangers that sojourned with him did the same" (*Life*, pp. 87–88).

This is a branch of the subject on which I do not use any urgency, because few have the gifts of Philip Henry or Cecil. There are, no doubt, many men who would find themselves less at home in the colloquial exposition of a chapter than in a labored discourse. While few things are better than a timely, judicious exposition, nothing can be worse than the opposite abuse. I dare not give an indiscriminate exhortation to the duty lest I subject some poor family to the infliction of tedious, ignorant, erroneous, or overheated harangues under the name of expounding Scripture at family-prayer. But where a Christian parent feels himself called to engage in this service, with due preparation and reliance on God, he may look for blessed results.

The manner of reading the Bible in the family is of great importance. My judgment is that too much care cannot be bestowed on this point. If anything should be well read, it is God's message. Half its meaning, and almost all its effect, are sometimes suffocated and lost by a sleepy, monotonous, stupid, careless, and inarticulate drawling, or, what is worse, an affected delivery.

For this reason, I am altogether convinced that the portion of Scripture should, in general, be wholly read by the head of the family. I often complain, with justice, of the interruption of the sense, occasioned by the breaking up of the passage into verses; but this evil is made tenfold worse when each verse is pronounced by a different person. However the mode of reading in rotation may seem to awaken attention, it is clearly injurious to the effect. No one would ever think of reading any secular paragraph of lively interest, such as a letter, or news from Europe, in this manner. It gives the solemn service too much the air of a school lesson, with all the worst annoyances of the school, such as the spelling out of words, mispronunciation, and mistakes, losing the place, and divers mishaps tending to the ludicrous. The solemn service of God should not be made a school lesson. Let each have his book, but let it be felt that Scriptures cannot be read too well by the best reader in the house; and there is a propriety in having it pronounced with all solemnity and expression, and without interruption, by him who has the reverence of all present. Such is my decided opinion which, however, I would not for a moment seek to impose as a yoke on that liberty which I dearly prize in all divine service.

It is so far from being a matter of indifference how, or by whom, the Scriptures shall be read in family worship that particular care should be bestowed on a due preparation for this work by every head of a family. Supposing him to be a man not familiar with every part of the Bible, there would be nothing amiss in his reading over with great attention, in private, the chapter to which he is about to attend with his family. No one need consider it beneath his dignity to make good reading his special study, not in the way of rhetorical rule and elocutionary tricks (far be it from us to recommend the emptiest of all pretenses!), but by fully understanding the language, and deeply entering into the spirit of the passage. At the fireside or in the pulpit, this will do more than all the orotund mouthing, and "start theatric, practiced at the glass." It has often been asserted that the reading of a chapter by the late Dr. John M. Mason was as good as another man's exposition; and I have heard a clergyman say that he would walk ten miles to hear Dean Kirwan repeat the Lord's Prayer. I have seldom felt the power of delivery more than in hearing Summerfield rehearse a passage of Scripture without comment (2 Corinthians 6:1-12). It is true, we cannot, with all our study, hope to be Kirwans, Masons, or Summerfields, but we may keep ourselves from being intolerably bad. From the acme of their elocution, there is an unbroken descent down to the halting, humdrum, listless, careless, and, therefore, profane manner in which the sacred oracles are sometimes read at family worship.

Bible distribution, now in so happy a progress, should lead to family Bible reading. Happy would be our nation if every house possessed not only the volume, but this use of it. It is not enough that we lay the volume at every man's door. We do not claim for it the virtue of a charm or talisman which shall save him who lies asleep. Though we strive to furnish the book, it is not the mere furnishing of the book which is to save the world. Yet the storehouse of medicine is not the less necessary because some will not use it. It is the book in which all have a common interest. It is the *only* such book. Since the great efforts made during our century for this object, certain high-church mockers have sneered at an alleged superstitious adoration of the Bible, which the objectors have been pleased to name "Bibliolatry." They have declared that the Word of God was more venerated and sought more eagerly when it was hard to reach, and when the massive folio of the sixteenth century used to be chained fast to a pillar in some English church. Now, while I acknowledge that a loaf of bread is more valued in a ship on short allowance, or in the famine of a siege, than on the tables of plenty, I am no less desirous that every man should have his loaf.

I bless God for handing down His precious Word not only by the church, but by the family. We have received it from our fathers, and we would transmit it to our latest posterity. Family instruction in the Scriptures goes very far back. "Thou shalt teach them diligently unto thy children, and shalt talk to them, when thou sittest down, and when thou walkest by the way, and when thou liest down, and when thou risest up. And thou shalt bind them for a sign upon thy hand, and they shall be as frontlets between thine eyes. And thou shalt write them upon the posts of thy house, and on thy gates" (Deuteronomy 6).

The modern Jews resemble the Papists in some things; but they have never become idolaters, and they have never withheld the Word of God from the laity. It has been read in every synagogue for centuries, and is so read to this hour. It is read in every Hebrew house every day. It is my hope that the day will come when at least as much as this may be said of Christians all over the world. Let us send down the Word of God to our descendants. When I look at the folio Bible which was my grandfather's, I cannot bear the thought that it should stop with me. Human generations change, but God's truth abides. "For all flesh is grass, and all the glory of man is like the flower of grass: the grass withereth, and the flower thereof falleth away; but the Word of the Lord endureth forever" (1 Peter 1:24–25). This is the Word which we desire may be read in the houses of our offspring when Christ shall appear.

15

Psalmody As a Part of Family Worship

Good Mr. Philip Henry used to say that the singing of God's people at family worship was a way to hold forth godliness to such as pass by their windows, like Rahab's scarlet thread (Joshua 2:17). Sacred song is an instituted means of giving expression to every high, religious emotion. It has been adopted for this purpose in every form of religion known among men. Concerning its fitness for this end in the great assembly, there has been no controversy in the church. Never was the glory of divine song more exalted than in the ancient temple service. It was at once admitted into the primitive assemblies, and has prevailed in all Christian churches. "In singing the praises of God," says *The Directory for Worship,* "we are to sing with the spirit, and with the understanding also; making melody in our hearts unto the Lord. It is also proper that we cultivate some knowledge of the rules of music, that we may praise God in a becoming manner with our voices as well as with our hearts" (Chapter 4. 2). There has been no difference of judgment on this point in any of the reformed churches. But I ask attention to the assertion that there is no argument for sacred music in the church which does not hold equally good in the family. Though this part of the service has fallen out of the practice of many households, and (strangely enough) extensively in those regions where scientific music has been most boastfully cultivated, the judgment of our church in its *Directory for Public Worship* on this

127

subject is explicit: "It is the duty of Christians to praise God, by singing psalms or hymns, publicly in the church, as also privately in the family" (Chapter 4. 1). There is no reason for one which is not a reason for the other. If a congregation has its joys and other elevated emotions, so has a family. If a congregation has cause to give utterance to these with "the voice of melody," so has a family. If a congregation has voices which are fitted for this work, so has a family. In truth, what is a family but a domestic congregation, or "church in the house?"

Domestic psalmody is promotive of devotion. It is an exercise in which the voices of all join in the expression of sentiments which should be experienced by all. I trust I shall not be called upon to prove that the singing of God's praise is eminently conducive to the awakening and maintenance of holy affections, and that it has been in every age employed by the Holy Spirit for this purpose. But I beg consideration of the statement that this is as true of the family as of the church. The peculiar exercises of soul which belong to families, as such, find expression in sacred song no less than those which belong to public assemblies. The godly sorrow, the trust, the adoration, and the thanks of a household seem to require this channel for their flow.

Psalmody is a means of Christian instruction. In the early church, many of the hymns were compendious formulas of doctrine; and such has been the case in every succeeding age. "Let the word of Christ dwell in you richly in all wisdom, teaching and admonishing one another, in psalms and hymns and spiritual songs, singing with grace in your hearts to the Lord" (Colossians 3:16). In this view, it is wise to seize upon sacred poetry as a means of fastening truth on the infant mind; and the daily practice of the family will, beyond anything else, familiarize the young with the choicest spiritual songs. In order that this may take place most fully, the selection should be careful; and the number of hymns so used should not be too large. Where so much depends on repetition, there may be an inordinate passion for variety. A small circle of well-adapted psalms and hymns is better than a great multitude, and the suggestion derives new importance from the extraordinary augmentation of our stock of religious compositions in verse.

The happy influence of spiritual songs is illustrated in the early churches of Germany. Luther was himself a poet and a musician; and he bestowed on his country many of her noblest hymns and some of her finest melodies. In his writings he often alludes to this as one of the chosen agencies in the work of Reformation; and this not merely in the church, but by the wayside and at home. He relates that, in the earliest part of his labors, he was moved to tears by hearing a wandering beggar under his window sing a hymn which has since become famous, but which Luther had never before heard. The remarkable cultivation of music among the United Brethren is only the extension by Zinzendorf of this attachment to sacred song, which was encouraged by Luther. The impress still remains. Wherever you meet a German Christian, you find him charged with those noble and evangelical compositions. Even the emigrant, in his blouse, is sure, if a disciple, to carry across the sea in his wallet the black-covered hymnbook.

The same thing is observable among our Presbyterian forefathers and their descendants in Scotland and Ireland. They praised God in their families. Usually having the metrical psalms at the end of their pocket Bibles, they were familiar with them from youth; and they held them in more reverence, conceiving them to be a literal version of the Word of God. While I condemn the narrowness of that prejudice which would debar the Church of God from naming the name of Christ in public praise, and which would reject all New Testament hymns, I cannot shut my eyes to the singular influence of that ancient version; though written by an Englishman, Francis Rouse or Rous, it has become almost the peculiar treasure of the Scots, and is still used in the Kirk of Scotland, and the Secession bodies of Britain and America.

This use of psalmody in family worship I believe to have been almost universal in the old Presbyterian church of Scotland, as it has been laudably kept up till this day. That it tended, in a high degree, to increase the interest of all concerned in the service, and to promote Christian knowledge and sound piety, I cannot for a moment doubt. The homely old version—with a small number of ancient airs of great plainness, severity, and sweetness, some of which still linger in our churches—was familiar to every man, woman, and child. The favorite poet of Scotland has not failed to seize on this trait in the family picture, to which, therefore, I once more call attention:

> They chant their artless notes in simple guise,
> They tune their hearts, by far their noblest aim,
> Perhaps Dundee's wild warbling measures rise,
> Or plaintive Martyrs, worthy of the name,
> Or noble Elgin beats the heavenward flame,
> The sweetest far of Scotia's holy lays.
> Compared with these Italian trills are tame;
> The tickled ears no heartfelt raptures raise,
> Nae unison hae they with our Creator's praise.

The Wesleyans in Great Britain, and their Methodist brethren in America, have beyond all others done justice to the animating power of sacred song in public and in the house; and we may learn a lesson from them. Differing from them as we do in several important points, we shall, nevertheless, always hold ourselves ready to give them just praise for the Christian vivacity of their services. And I hazard whatever may be at stake of reputation for taste when I say that, after some opportunities of listening to what is regarded as the choicest music which has come to us from abroad, I have felt more of the genuine power of harmonious sounds when the voices of "the great congregation" have united in sending up a volume of song than from orchestral clangor, or the artistic combinations of stringed instruments and organs.

It is a remarkable fact that in those circles of the religious world which consider themselves the most accomplished, there are many families where sacred music receives no separate attention. We enter the saloons of wealth, professedly consecrated to God, and our eyes are greeted by the piano-forte, the guitar, the organ, or the harp, and by piles of complicated and fashionable music. But when the hour of family worship arrives, no hymn of praise ascends to God. Those cultivated voices, so cunning in solfeggio and Italian trills, are dumb for all but this world's song. Our Christian daughters, practicing for hours a day under great masters of singing, are sometimes unwilling to lend their aid even in the house of God. I solemnly commend this subject to those who preside over the education of youth.

Some are ready to say that psalmody cannot be maintained with ease in domestic worship, because in many instances a majority of those present are children. It is strange that this objection should arise at the very period in which, above all that have preceded, juvenile instruction in music has been pursued with success. The concurrent testimony of all who have most largely examined and experimented on the matter is that no child has been found (unless in case of organic defect) who could not be taught to sing. No school of the higher class ventures to exclude vocal music from its course of study. Not a word need be said concerning this to such as are familiar with the extraordinary labors of Mr. Hastings, or have attended the public exhibitions of Mr. Bradbury and others, in some of which no less than five hundred children have appeared at once in the admirable performance of the most celebrated compositions of the great masters. A much simpler cultivation would suffice for all that we require.

Family worship affords the most happy means of bringing forward infant voices in the praise of God. I have known children who joined, without false intonation, in the family psalm before they could distinctly articulate a word. It is almost always an attractive and delightful part of the worship to youthful minds, and hence contributes to endear the household meeting and the circle of home. Above all, it makes this early impression, that the voice is to be trained for the glory of God as its best and happiest office.

The use of psalmody in domestic worship tends to the improvement of this part of divine service in public. We may push the art and exquisite harmony of choirs or select companies to any degree of advancement, however high, yet the great end will not be attained until we secure the united voices of the whole congregation. Every method which discourages or postpones this, however agreeable to human taste, is a snare which should be deprecated. So long as great numbers in the body of a church feel at liberty to dispute this part of religion to others, the worship of God is abridged of its rightful claim. I believe that the revival of psalmody in the house would contribute to train voices for the sanctuary.

In order to have this effect, it should not be left to take care of itself or be executed in a careless, random way. Some pains should be taken to select suitable tunes, and to make every member of the household familiar with them. This might be done by means of an occasional hour of musical instruction, such as is implied in the injunction which we have already cited from our *Directory*. But the daily exercise itself is a school of music; and I have never known a family in which it was common, that did not attain to some excellence in this department.

Conscientious regard to the spiritual aspect of divine praise will lead him who presides in family worship to look upon the selection of appropriate psalms and hymns as a matter of great importance. He will not leave it to accident, but from the ample stores which we possess will endeavor to choose such as may both be level to the capacity of his little flock and suited to carry up their hearts directly to God. These sacred compositions, I hope, will rest in the memory of our children when we shall be no more with them. No evil can arise from often recurring to the same hymns, if these are in themselves excellent. The best hymns are those which are sung most often, and which everyone knows by heart; and those will have the largest stock in remembrance who have praised God all their lives at home. I do not understand the feelings of that man who can ever weary of such compositions as those which begin thus: "My God, my life, my love" . . . "Alas! and did my Savior bleed" . . . "Not all the blood of beasts" . . . "Come we, who love the Lord" . . . "My God, the spring of all my joys" . . . "When I can read my title clear" . . . "There is a land of pure delight" . . . "Plunged in a gulf of dark despair" . . . "The Lord my Shepherd is" . . . "Teach me the measure of

my days" . . . "When overwhelmed with grief" . . . "Lord of
the worlds above" or "Sweet is the work, my God, my
King." Such psalms and hymns, so far from losing by repetition, gain new associations day by day: and I venture to
assert that they are sung by none in the house of God with
so much real delight as by the aged man who lays aside his
spectacles because the psalm has been known to him for
forty years.

No religious duty can be conducted aright unless the
heart is in it; and there are special reasons why the thoughts
and affections should be tempted to wander in the singing
of God's praise. How few, even in the largest worshipping
assemblies, show, by their demeanor that the words which
are on their lips, or on the lips of their substitutes in the
work of praise, are addressed to the present and heart-
searching Jehovah! The soul may be entirely taken up in the
secular and musical part of the psalmody. No pains can be
too great which may result in the awakening of solemn
consideration in the minds of those who join in singing
praise. Every symptom of levity should be repressed. An occasional remark, if solemnly and appropriately thrown in
before engaging in this duty, might often have a good effect. It is an offense against God to address Him in words
of high moment while, perhaps, we have no thought of
their meaning, still less any sympathy with their sentiment.
Each of us should learn to say with sincerity, "I will sing
with the spirit, I will sing with the understanding also"
(1 Corinthians 14:15).

It would be a peculiar pleasure to this writer if he could
know that he had succeeded in bringing the vocal praise of
God into the daily worship of even a single household.
Those who make the experiment will find a new spring of
delight gushing out under the domestic vine and figtree.

They will rejoice in a fresh sweetener of their toils and anxieties, and a powerful instrument for quieting and training the souls of their children. It is mournful to think that a service which was so precious to our ancestors, and which they made sacrifices to enjoy, even when under the sword of persecution, should die out of many Christian families in these days of peace when there is no lack of worldly rejoicings, "and the harp, and the viol, the tabret, and pipe, and wine, are in their feasts" (Isaiah 5:12). There may be days in which we have scarcely the heart to sing by reason of deep anguish, but such are not the days of most. "Is any merry? Let him sing psalms" (James 5:13). Before we totally hush the voice of thanksgiving in our tabernacle, let us break or banish the instruments of worldly music. No law can be laid down for those who have not the control of their own time, or those who, after every effort, are convinced that it is impossible for them to sing; but I would advise a shortening of the other services rather than the total omission of this. Such as have abundance of leisure should honor God by the psalm, and "make the voice of His praise to be heard" (Psalm 66:8).

16

The Householder Exhorted to the Duty of Family Worship

Every portion of what has preceded has tended to the single point of inducing the reader to maintain the worship of God in his house; but it is desirable to make the appeal even more closely and, as it were, personally to the heart and conscience. Laying aside therefore, all more ceremonious modes of approach, I would respectfully and affectionately address myself to the individual professor of religion.

You are, by Providence, set at the head of a family to support it, instruct it, guard it, and in every way care for its temporal and eternal good. I offer to you a simple means of contributing to the greatest of these objects; and I have at some length dwelled upon its excellencies and fruits. My plea is for those whom you love the best, for your own flesh and blood. No human language can well go beyond the importance of the domestic relation. On this point you require no prompting. When you return from the toils and distractions of the day, and sit at home amidst the little quiet circle, you feel that you are among your chief wealth. This is your treasure. The law makes it your castle, and religion may make it your sanctuary. As your eye rests on the wife of your bosom, and the pledges of your mutual love, you silently give thanks to God; and sometimes your heart overflows in earnest wishes for the good of each beloved object. Withhold not a single defense or ornament from that

Christian home which is already the source of so many virtues and enjoyments.

> Domestic happiness, thou only bliss
> Of Paradise that has survived the fall!
> Though few now taste thee unimpaired and pure,
> Or tasting, long enjoy thee! too infirm,
> Or too incautious to preserve thy sweets
> Unmixed with drops of bitter, which neglect
> Or temper sheds into thy crystal cup;
> Thou art the nurse of Virtue, in thine arms
> She smiles, appearing, as in truth she is,
> Heaven-born, and destined to the skies again. (Cowper)

If you would preserve these sweets, connect them with heaven. Have you no desire to honor God in the midst of His favors? Do you see no seemliness in recognizing the religion of Christ in your family capacity? Even supposing that there were no injunction of such a service as this, one might expect it to grow up spontaneously in Christian households. Prayer is a duty of natural religion. The Mohammedan, wherever he journeys, prays to God five times a day, at his stated hours. The very heathen, in their families, call on their gods "which are yet not gods" (Jeremiah 2:11). Shall a Christian house be void of all tokens of its relation to God? One might claim of you, as a follower of the Redeemer, to hold forth some such sign that, as for you and your house, you fear the Lord (Joshua 24:15). If God had given no indications of His good pleasure in this ordinance, it is one of so great value and blessedness, that we might all reasonably join in asking it at His hands as a special boon. But He gives it to us freely; and yet the heavenly gift is spurned by thousands! Suppose it were revealed to us that we were forbidden to worship

God in our families. Though all other means should remain undiminished, it would be a fearful interdict, a portentous curfew to our domestic fires. The parent and the child could no longer press around the feet of divine mercy, clinging more closely because the rest of the world is shut out. Yet multitudes deny themselves all this blessing of their own free choice; and parents and children grow up and live and separate and appear in judgment without having ever met, even once, in an act of common household supplication! It is amazing, and all but incredible, that any man who loves Christ should be willing to preside over a family in which, from year to year, there is nothing to signalize it as belonging to the Lord.

O Christian parent! "Suffer the word of exhortation." Be persuaded not to deny your comforts. The principle is undoubted that we have tenfold pleasure in that which we enjoy in company with those whom we love. That is not a father's heart which does not experience it everyday. We realize it in our common meals, our recreations, our readings, our excursions, and our visits; why should you not realize it in your religion? Family worship is a coming to God not singly, but hand-in-hand with your children and family; and from this peculiar aspect it has delights and advantages which are all its own.

The family, as such, has its wants and dangers, its sorrows and sins, which it is, therefore, reasonable to lay before God in a special devotion. No human community stands out from the mass in such substantive and prominent individuality; the circle which bounds it is clear and sharply marked, and has been described by the hand of God Himself. There is a community of interest; no persons on earth are so much bound together. Nothing can befall anyone without reaching the whole circle. You are invited to present your household, as a household, before the infinite Giver of all good. Be assured that He will make a distinction between those who fear Him and those who fear Him not. It was with a dreadful reference to this very family tie that God said, "Them that honor Me I will honor, and they that despise Me shall be lightly esteemed" (1 Samuel 2:30). Your habitation will be more safe, and its inmates more prosperous, by reason of God's answer to the petitions which you put up together.

By a faithful observance of family worship, you will be employing a daily means towards the eternal salvation of your household. It is scarcely possible to think of this without some impression. The everlasting damnation of your own offspring is a catastrophe so awful that no single instrument which promises to avert it should be omitted. No prayers, indeed, considered as so much work wrought, will effectually save these souls; but I know of no means which tend more directly to this end than domestic worship, and the duties to which it leads. Are you willing to hazard so great a neglect? Dare you live any longer, withholding yourself from an agency which adds even a hair's weight of probability to the eventual rescue of these beloved, perishing souls? There are other means, indeed, but they are seldom used by the neglecters of family prayer. Think how hard you already find the performance of these duties; how your mouth is closed, in regard to the personal admonition of your children and servants; how little you have spoken to them of their sin and danger, and of the way of salvation by Christ; how defective your example is; how few tokens you give them of such a power and loveliness in religion as may draw them to it. You assuredly are not so rich in spiritual agency on your little flock as to be able to do without this. If humbly attempted and devoutly pursued, there is good reason to believe that it will result in their eternal good. I put it to your conscience, in the sight of God, whether you can despise it without exceeding guilt.

You need the aid of family worship in the rearing of your children; this has been discussed at large. Your duty is now to act upon the truth. At present, while your children, perhaps, are small, you find government an easy task. They reverently hear your words, pray by your side, and weep at the name of Jesus; you are sometimes tempted to think their hearts renewed. But a few years will make a strange difference. Let them enter upon adolescence, and all your cords will prove like the spider's web unless you shall have maintained your influence upon them by the daily-growing bond of family religion. Look around you, among families professing faith in Christ, and observe the difference between those who worship God and those who do not; and then, as you love your offspring, and as you would save them from the rebellion of Hophni and Phinehas, set up the worship of God in your house.

Family worship has been shown to be a happy instrument for the promotion of piety in a household. A true Christian will desire that his children and dependents should be not merely safe, but eminently holy. Are you conscious of any such desires? In the absence of them, can you persuade yourself that you are a child of God? Or, feeling them, can you possibly endure a life without so much as one common prayer as a family? Have you no call for domestic thanksgiving? No daily mercies? No special deliverances? No long-continued exemptions from evil? It is monstrous that a Christian household should be absolutely dumb on these points. I scarcely know how it can be so. Some tribute of gratitude will surely burst forth, unawares, and ascend to heaven from a sanctified dwelling. "The voice of rejoicing and salvation is in the tabernacles of the righteous" (Psalm 118:15).

God has, I suppose, given you a number of children. They are "an heritage of the Lord," and "the fruit of the womb is his reward. As arrows are in the hand of a mighty man, so are children of thy youth; happy is the man that hath his quiver full of them. They shall not be ashamed, but they shall speak with the enemies in the gate" (Psalm 127:3–5). But that you may enjoy such blessings, it is indispensable that you should be living in the performance of parental duty, and especially that you should be engaged in prayer with your little ones. In a prayerless dwelling, children seem to stretch out their little hands to the professing father for this needful protection and benediction, as really as the helpless brood regards the parent bird for natural supplies.

It is dreadful to consider the neglect of family worship, as connected with the engagements implied in infant baptism. In that sacrament, the parents solemnly dedicate their little one to God, the Father, the Son, and the Holy Ghost, and do as solemnly incur an obligation to use all methods for the accomplishment of that which is set forth in the rite. The officiating minister is directed to exhort parents to carefully perform their duty, requiring them to instruct their child, "that they pray with and for it; that they set an example of piety and godliness before it; and endeavor, by all the means of God's appointment, to bring up their child in the nurture and admonition of the Lord" (*Directory for Worship*, 7. 4). It is a matter of very general usage, though not expressly enjoined by our church, to exact from parents a solemn vow in regard to this particular duty. I remain in wonder by what means so many professing parents absolve themselves from this affecting obligation.

You are, it may be, the head of a family which has numerous domestics and other dependents, whose souls are entrusted to your care. Here is a means of daily appearing before them in a religious character, and daily drawing their thoughts to divine things. Little as it may have burdened your conscience, it will enter into that judgment which awaits you. And unless you have arrived at some better way of inculcating truth and promoting piety, and unless you are in the active observance of a better method, you cannot, without sin, neglect the domestic worship of God.

With particular and affectionate earnestness I would commend this subject to young householders who are just entering on domestic life for themselves. The marriage bond is too often contracted with a predominance of worldly and dissipating thoughts, if not with great levity. But there are serious associations to a reflecting mind hovering around the union of two young persons for life. And here, as in other things, first steps are momentous. Begin aright, and you escape some of the most formidable difficulties in the way of this observance. Sanctify the union of your hearts by the institution of God's service. Resolve that as soon as you have a house, you will have your Lord acknowledged under its roof. This will sweeten every solace of your days. The time is near when you shall feel your need of it. It will give a color to your whole life. Especially in days of affliction (and they will come), you will have at hand a spring of divine comforts. Honor God in the beginning of your course, and when you approach its close you will bless His holy name that He ever put the thought into your heart.

You are, perhaps, a new professor, but just admitted to the table of the Lord. You are at the best juncture for amending what is evil in your life. Let no delays prevent your immediate enjoyment of this ordinance. Break through every restraint, and let the time of your public avouching of God as your God be marked by your solemn and deliberate establishment of God's worship in your dwelling. Such is your obvious duty, if you have failed up to the time of a profession of faith. But let not these remarks be interpreted as if the duty of family prayer were dependent on the sacramental communion. So far from it, that even if you have never united yourself in the full enjoyment of church fellowship you are no less bound to honor God in your own house this very day. But he who, after struggles of mind in regard to other duties, can deliberately approach the Lord's table, and then go home and resume a course of heathenish forgetfulness of domestic worship, must be regarded as diseased in conscience, if not altogether misled as to his personal acceptance.

It is a delicate question, which is often proposed to ministers of the gospel, whether those who make no public profession of their faith should be encouraged in the maintenance of family worship. In replying to it, I desire to speak with modesty, and yet with decision. The two duties are not dependent on one another. Family prayer is a duty of every householder, binding on him every day of his life. The believing remembrance of Christ at His table is another duty. Where a man who is grave and sober, and who has been trained in the ways of God, is prompted to honor his Creator and Benefactor in his dwelling, I dare not forbid him, any more than I would forbid him to pray in his closet. I would employ the occasion to urge upon him the grand, paramount duty of faith in the Lord Jesus, and the duty of publicly professing such faith; but I would likewise rejoice to see him, without delay, assembling his household for the worship of the Lord. Let him be warned of the danger of resting in such means, or in any means; let him not hope by such performance to propitiate that divine favor which come only on the believing; let him not delay an instant to fly to the mercy of God in Jesus Christ; but let him, nevertheless, conduct his children and servant to that throne of grace where sovereign grace may vouchsafe to him an undeserved benefit. Nay, while I would sedulously avoid seeming to compound for a greater duty by the performance of a lesser, I do not hesitate to say that, where more cannot be secured, it is an act of Christian mercy to households to prevail on their head even to read a chapter in the Bible, morning and evening.

It may be said to some that you have pursued the tenor of your way in the utter neglect of family worship. To you, the message is simple: fly at once, with your household, to the throne of grace! Cease to consider it as a matter of indifference, or an affair of variable custom. The neglect is most serious. It is your loss, and the loss of your offspring. It is your sin. It calls for repentance and for reformation, which is the criterion of repentance. Instead of a lingering meditation on the expediency of the work, you should begin now. "To him that knoweth to do good, and doeth it not, to him it is sin" (James 4:17).

17

Difficulties, Objections, and Conclusion

The fact that an observance so important and fruitful should be widely disregarded, even in Protestant churches, may well give rise to serious inquiry into the causes of such neglect. Misapprehensions, objections, and difficulties must certainly exist, or we should find it as universal as Sabbath-worship.

Laying aside all flattering words, I may say plainly that I regard the neglect of family worship as springing from lukewarmness and worldliness in religion, and as a portentous evil of our day. Where piety is ardent and operative, it cannot but diffuse itself through the domestic structure. Where a man has the spirit of prayer, he will naturally be led to give vent to his devotion in fellowship with those whom he loves most of all on earth. I am ready to make allowance for the force of long habit, and the religious usages of particular countries, and will not hastily condemn those who, in the midst of popery and neology, are governed by the customs of their vicinity. But even there I have already observed that as vital godliness advances, this service, or something equivalent, comes in by a natural suggestion, or rather by a suggestion of grace. And where the custom of Protestant churches abroad, in any region, authorizes the disuse of domestic prayer, I do not hesitate to refer the origin of this disuse to the decay of piety in a former age. I have good reason to believe that all the Reformation churches were acquainted with family prayer.

A great accession to the piety of a Christian house will manifest itself in nothing more speedily than in the necessity under which they will feel themselves laid to come together in acts of worship. There may be persons who know not what it is. For one large class, however, no such apology can be made. They are sons of the church, introduced within its guardian care by baptism, and familiarized to the daily sanctuary of which they can even now scarcely hear or think without recalling the image of a sainted father whose voice in their early years conducted them to the praise of God. When such persons, so instructed, establish households of their own, with a daily memento of their youthful privilege and their present neglect in every hour at which God was wont to be worshipped under the paternal roof, and still deny the faith of their childhood, they not only sin, but sin knowingly and inexcusably. Nothing but the absence of devout affections can account for such a life.

So great is my desire, however, to meet the neglecters of this service on any ground that I will yield a ready attention to all their doubts, scruples, and objections; and for this purpose no better way suggests itself than that of supposing the replies which may be made to my preceding urgent beseeching that the reader would enter upon family worship forthwith. What arguments can we imagine from his lips?

OBJECTION 1. "The service, as I see it, is a dull formality; and my house is well off without it."

RESPONSE. Then you have seen it under great neglect or perversion. Like all religious services, it may be so conducted as to be both dull and formal. But no Christian observance known among men admits of more life, and none is connected with more sources of tender affection. Very ignorant, very stupid, or very irreligious people may transform it into a tedious and burdensome routine, but this is no fault of the ordinance. They do the same with every sacred thing they touch. I do not invite you to such a service, or to any dead formality, but to that which, under the influence of elevated emotion, may be made, and is daily made, a delightful and animating means of grace. True, it is simple, and lacks all the paraphernalia, posture, and grimace of anti-Christian rites; but in the households of the righteous it shines with a pure and hallowed attraction. And I appeal to those who have enjoyed it from their infancy, whether they do not regard it in retrospect with every feeling rather than that of weariness. Nay, the very reason why I would introduce this means under every roof is that it possesses in so remarkable a degree the quality of inspiring the liveliest emotion.

OBJECTION 2. "Family worship may be well enough in itself, but it does not fall in with the customs of my house and my guests."

RESPONSE. This is, with some, a valid argument, and it must be admitted that there are customs of households and of society with which family worship will assuredly interfere. Such is the custom of late and irregular rising—agreeably to which the yawning inmates of a house straggle down to a breakfast table which stands for hours, awaiting the successive approaches of the solitary and moody participant—and that other custom of passing a long evening, as it is called by the courtesy of fashion, at the theater, the card-party, the ball, or the no less unseasonable supper or assembly. It is not the least of the advantages of domestic prayer that it stands in open daily protest against these growing observances of the mode.

OBJECTION 3. "I have no time for family worship."

RESPONSE. In the hurry of our great cities, it is painful to observe the preference given to mammon over

God. Look at the living tide which rolls every morning down such a thoroughfare as Broadway! A stranger might be forgiven if he supposed that the life of each breathless banker, merchant, or clerk depended on his reaching the commercial latitudes within a certain minute. But how many of these have prayed with their families? Some, I rejoice to believe; but the mass have no time for anything but the world. Unless men will lose their own souls, and jeopard the souls of their children, they must take time for God. And the more busy, exhausting, and absorbing any man's days are, the more he needs the deliberate abstraction of a quiet devotional hour, such as that of family worship.

Samuel Davies wrote against this objection: "Were you formed for this world only, there would be some force in the objection; but how strange such an objection sounds in the heir of an eternity! Pray, what is your time given to you for? Is it not principally that you may prepare for eternity? And have you no time for what is the great business of your lives? Again, why do you not plead too that you have no time for your daily meals? Is food more necessary to your bodies than religion to your souls? If you think so, what has become of your understandings? Further, what employment do you follow? Is it lawful or unlawful? If unlawful, then renounce it immediately; if lawful, then it will admit of the exercise of family-religion, for God cannot command contradictions. And since He has commanded you to maintain His worship in your houses, that is demonstration that every calling which He allows you to follow will afford time for it. Finally, may you not redeem as much time from idle conversation, from trifling [from the morning papers], or even from your sleep, as may be sufficient for family religion? May you not order your family devotion so that your domestics may attend upon it, either before they go out to their work, or when they come to their meals?"

OBJECTION 4. "Our family is so small."

RESPONSE. How many are there of you? Are there two? Then, "wheresoever two or three are gathered together in My name . . ." (see Matthew 18:19–20). John Howard and his valet, as they journeyed from place to place, used to have family worship by themselves if they could get no one else to join them. "Wherever I have a tent," he would say, "there God shall have an altar." If there are two of you, though it is but a Ruth and a Naomi, a mother and her daughter, your family is large enough to worship God, and to get the blessing of those who worship Him.

OBJECTION 5. "My family is so large; there are so many servants, and so many visitors, that I have no courage to begin."

RESPONSE. "If your family is large, the obligation to begin is all the greater. Many suffer by your neglect. And if your congregation is numerous, the likelihood that some good will be done is the greater, for there are more to share the benefit. And why lack courage? Should not the very fact that you are acknowledging God encourage you? 'Them that honor Me, I will honor.' Begin it believingly, and in the very attempt courage will come" (Hamilton's *Church in the Home*).

OBJECTION 6. "There are persons present in my house whose superior age or intelligence deters me from the duty."

RESPONSE. To this it must be replied that if such persons are sober, wise, and generous, they will look not only with allowance, but with kindly regard on the endeavor; and if they are otherwise, it is too much to demand of an independent and a Christian man that he should for an instant be governed by their caprices or their censure.

The head of a family should assert his authority in his own house.

OBJECTION 7. "I am unlearned and destitute of gifts."

RESPONSE. Either misapprehension or pride suggests this objection. It is not a service which demands genius, erudition, or eloquence. You have education enough to read a portion of the Scriptures with propriety and solemnity. And you can so far gather your thoughts by suitable pre-meditation as to pour out a prayer to God for those whom you love, which will be all the better for its simplicity of expression. The families are few in which the father needs to tremble before his own dependents. Then consider that the gift of prayer is from above, and that He who aids in the closet will aid in the family group. Unless, indeed, you labor under the evil consciousness that you are living in the neglect even of secret prayer, and then, as you have an additional sin to repent of, so you have an additional duty to perform. "What," says President [Samuel] Davies, "have you enjoyed preaching, Bibles, and good books so long, and yet do not know what to ask of God? Alas! what have you been doing?"

OBJECTION 8. "My family is unwilling to unite in the service."

RESPONSE. This is one of the worst things which can be testified of a family. Graceless, indeed, must those sons or daughters be who could for an instant hesitate to accompany their father to the throne of grace, or who could throw any obstacle in the way of such an observance. You have strangely neglected the maintenance of parental authority if any such temper really exists. The objection speaks loudly in favor of an early institution of family prayer that children may be accustomed to it from their earliest years, and not need to be reconciled to the holy custom after a long career of wayward folly. But granting that the mortifying case is as you have alleged, it is only a new proof that you should vindicate your claim as a Christian householder to rule in your own house.

OBJECTION 9. "The truth is, I am ashamed to begin."

RESPONSE. I seriously believe that this single reason operates with more force than all the others put together; and it is one with which I am constrained to deal honestly and solemnly. Men who have allowed their households to increase around them, without any visible service of God, awake to some sense of their duty, and would attempt the performance of it but for a secret dread of the sneer, even of a child or a servant. Religion frequently brings men to such a dilemma, and it is a test of sincerity. If the scorn of the world is to decide our conduct, we might as well abandon all service of God at once; but we know the lot of these who are ashamed of Christ. I choose to place the question on this ground, because true piety will lead a man to serve God in spite of shame. But in reality, the danger is, for the most part, one of the imagination. No such ridicule will commonly ensue, but rather inward approval and increased respect. And that feeling of strangeness which accompanies the entrance on an unaccustomed work will wear off, perhaps after the very first trial.

Among these and similar objections which might be stated, I have not found one which really goes against the duty itself, or which contravenes the reasons heretofore given in this book. I am therefore bound to press the immediate performance of the duty upon every sincere reader in the assurance that, so doing, he will bless God for having enabled him to enter upon so delightful a service. The days of life are few. Children are rapidly growing into their habits for life. Some of them will soon be beyond your reach. Death will, before long, work strange separations. The night comes. In prospect of that judgment which is nearly impending, be persuaded to lay aside all frivolous excuses, to take up the cross, and to be in your family, as well as elsewhere, a devout and unflinching servant of Christ.

Before removing my hand from these humble labors, I must be allowed to add that there are duties to be performed by those also who have never neglected the outward observance. To be what I have represented, family worship must be something more than a form of recurring service—however grave, punctual, or decorous. It may degenerate into a rite as empty as the sprinkling of holy water, the recounting of beads, or the putting on of phylacteries. Under the agency of infinite grace, it is a mighty instrument for good; but we must concentrate every power to bring out all its strength. No care can be too great which shall make this daily service more seemly, more solemn, more instructive, more interesting, and more affectionate. We should prepare for it by preparing the heart. We should earnestly and everyday make a deliberate and distinct effort to free ourselves from that apathy and that formality which attach themselves to a customary service. We should come to it with eagerness and love, and should endeavor, by God's help, so to conduct it as to show to all in the house that it is a delight, and that our heart's desire is that all may find it a delight. We should regard it as a daily avenue to the very feet of our God and Savior, and in this light as a privilege beyond all price. Like the kindred observance of the Sabbath (with which it commonly stands or falls), family worship is observed to be most delightful to those who bestow the most pains upon it.

We are too much disposed to rest satisfied with our avoiding the sin of those who altogether neglect domestic prayer. But how do we render it? Are we in earnest? Are we full of faith? Do our affections flow forth in it? Do we shun all undue haste? Is our deportment such, when engaged in this service, that all around us may bear testimony that it is a sincere tribute of our affections to God? Questions such as these may carry a rebuke to many householders. Perhaps one great cause of that declension of piety which we so generally lament in our country is connected with the nonperformance, or the ill performance, of this household duty. While we content ourselves with vague complaints, and wait for some reviving measures from abroad, here is a home-measure which is at every man's door. So long as every family spies out the sins of every other, and bewails the coldness of the body at large, the evil only grows; but if each family, in reliance on God, were to awake to the duties of domestic piety, household discipline and instruction and daily prayer, we would behold a gracious revival in all our churches. By the former method, no one house is benefited; by the latter, every house would become a Bethel. When shall we see among us that deeply-pervading national interest in divine things, which animated all classes in Scotland at the second Reformation? Mingled, as it doubtless was, with much misapprehension in regard to the connection of Christ's kingdom with the civil polity, it was, nevertheless, a genuine fire, infinitely to be preferred to the tepid languors of our American condition in divine things. Nor can we hope for a restitution of this until religion and the service of God is made the great business of every house. "Turn us, O God of our salvation, and cause Thine anger toward us to cease. Wilt Thou be angry with us forever? Wilt Thou draw out Thine anger to all generations? Wilt

Thou not revive us again, that Thy people may rejoice in Thee" (Psalm 85:4–6).